Puddings & Pies

Puddings & Pies

TRADITIONAL DESSERTS FOR A NEW GENERATION

BARBARA J. GRUNES

YANKEE BOOKS

Camden, Maine

Cover and text design by *Amy Fischer*, Camden, Maine

Cover photographs by *Ralph Copeland*, Thomaston, Maine

Food styling by *Kristie T. Scott*, Lincolnville Beach, Maine

Typeset by *Typeworks*, Belfast, Maine

Printed and bound in the United States

Library of Congress Cataloging-in-Publication Data

Grunes, Barbara.
    Puddings and pies : traditional desserts for new generations / by
Barbara J. Grunes.
      p.   cm.
    Includes index.
    ISBN 0-89909-329-9
    1. Puddings. 2. Pies. I. Title.
TX773.G74 1991
641.8'64 – dc20   91-11179
                                                      CIP

10 9 8 7 6 5 4 3 2 1

To my friend
MAGGIE HILDEBRANDT
of London, England

CONTENTS

INTRODUCTION

While the childhood cry "What's for dessert?" may not be sounded in adulthood (probably only out of a conscious avoidance of self-confession) Americans are certainly a nation of dessert lovers. Dessert marks the pinnacle of the meal. No course produces the anticipation, elicits the oohs and ahs, and affords the satisfaction as a dessert.

The most inventive and expansive realm in recent American cooking is surely the dessert dish. For various reasons, American home cooks are exploring and turning their creative attentions to a wide spectrum of desserts, from old-fashioned and classic desserts to new, rich, and elegant desserts and finally to lighter and more healthful desserts. Contrasting motivations appear to have emerged in dessert planning and preparation. The nostalgic with the innovative, the simple and basic with the glamorous and exotic, the richer and heavier with the lighter and more diet conscious.

I have created this dessert cookbook to serve these varying interests and desires, while at the same time providing basic, simple, yet glorious recipes in two of the most popular of all dessert categories, puddings and pies. The pudding and pie recipes included in this book encompass a strong British/Early New England tradition and combine a classic and historic dessert custom with the techniques and capabilities of the modern American kitchen.

The pudding section was inspired by a treasured gift from a dear friend some years ago. I am indebted to Maggie Hildebrandt, whose mother grew up in the Cotswold area of southwestern England during the early twentieth century. She was for a time a dancing instructor to royalty, and her experiences combined the rural simplicity of Cotswold with the elegance of court life. Maggie Hildebrandt, knowing my lifelong obsession with recipes and cooking, was kind enough to give me two hand-written cookbooks compiled by her mother. These cookbooks are rich in English culinary tradition, and I have been particularly intrigued and enchanted by her recipes for both English pudding and pies. While the handwritten recipes evoke a nostalgic journey back to a more simplified and leisurely time, I have interpreted these recipes liberally, in light of the changes and innovations in the New England kitchen.

Puddings & Pies

PUDDINGS

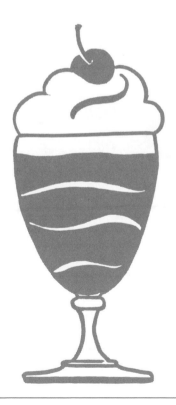

PUDDINGS

Pudding Time \ the time when pudding or puddings are to be had; hence, a time when one is in luck; a favorable or useful time.

The Oxford English Dictionary

In 1690, a French visitor to England, Misson de Valbourg, sang the paean for the most cherished of English dishes:

> Blessed be he that invented pudding! Ah, what an excellent thing is an English pudding! To come in pudding time, is . . . to come in the most lucky moment in the world.

It is certainly pudding that marks the paragon of English cooking.

The origin of pudding belongs to the British Isles, although the French, considering all realms of cuisine to be their own inventive domain, have tried to lay claim to that prized honor. The Saxons probably deserve the credit for creating the first type of pudding, batter pudding, and it is certain that various puddings, sweetened with honey, were a popular and common dish in England well before the Norman Conquest. The variety of and use of puddings, both as a dessert dish and as a main course, evolved dramatically throughout English history, reaching its height during the reign of Queen Victoria, the "golden age" of English pudding.

The pleasures of puddings have never diminished in England; even today in England, the term *pudding* covers a much wider range than we would traditionally associate with the term in America. "What's for pudding?" refers to the entire gamut of sweet desserts that follow the main course of an English meal, revealing the depth and powerful influence of pudding in English culinary history.

When the English settled the Atlantic coast in America, they brought the pudding tradition with them and quickly adapted it to native foods. In both New England and the South, cooks made corn puddings. Yankee Hasty Pudding was merely boiled cornmeal with seasonings. Indian puddings were sweet, baked puddings with maple syrup. As the country expanded, pudding became a standard dinner fare, as its flexibility and variety made it highly adaptable to both the growing cities of the East and South and the harsh conditions of the frontier.

In this section, I have presented four types of puddings – steamed puddings, baked puddings and custards, cooked puddings, and what I like to call "Name" puddings, which are unique puddings with imaginative and funny names. There are hundreds of types of puddings and pudding recipes available to the modern cook; I have included both classic puddings and a number of new pudding recipes that I think will work marvelously in American kitchens.

Today, puddings are becoming increasingly popular as a dessert dish, affording a range from rich, elegant, sauce-covered productions, to fruit puddings that embrace the full array of fall bounty, and finally to the light, creamy desserts that can be a perfect culmination to a heavy meal. The flexibility of pudding desserts, in terms of preparation, taste and flavor, and ingredient choice, is truly amazing.

Puddings have always made a perfect winter dessert, but light summer puddings are equally divine. The fruit puddings that utilize the harvests of late summer and autumn give a terrific alternative to fruit pies. Finally, holiday puddings, particularly plum pudding, the most glorious of all Christmas dishes, are a truly integral part of the holiday meal, treasured and anticipated by all.

STEAMED PUDDINGS

Steamed puddings are a traditional favorite, and their popularity is now returning in kitchens across the country. Steamed puddings are very easy to prepare, and they can be cooked ahead of time and frozen for months before reheating and serving.

Steamed puddings tend to be denser and more cake-like than baked and stove-top puddings. They are customarily served with a sauce that will complement the pudding. It is a good idea to prepare the sauce while the pudding is steaming.

Although many early puddings called for the use of suet, I have eliminated the use of suet in all but a few recipes. You may substitute butter, margarine, or vegetable shortening for suet in any pudding recipes.

Steamed puddings may be cooked in a variety of pudding molds, glazed ceramic molds, metal pudding molds. A pudding mold is a worthwhile investment if you plan to have steamed puddings in your cooking repertoire. If the mold you use does not have a tight-fitting lid, you must cover the top of the mold very tightly, using heavy or double-thickness of buttered or oiled foil. Do not hesitate to construct your own steamer. A large deep pan, large enough to hold the mold and steamer rack, and a tight-fitting cover are all that you need. The pan must be large enough to allow for good circulation of the steam around the mold.

The insides and lid of the mold should be greased liberally. Fill the mold only three-quarters full with the prepared pudding ingredients to allow for expansion. To prevent air bubbles and compact the pudding mixture, tap the mold several times.

To steam the pudding, use a large steamer or a heavy kettle or pot with a close-fitting lid. The steamer or pot must be large enough to allow for good circulation of the steam around the mold. Place the mold on a steaming rack at the bottom of the steamer or pot. Fill the steamer with enough water to reach approximately halfway up the mold. Remove the mold and bring the water to a boil. Return the mold to the pot of boiling water and tightly cover the pot. Reduce heat to simmer. Steam the pudding for the required length of time, checking occasionally. Add boiling water if necessary during the steaming time. Remember to use extreme caution when lifting the lid of the kettle. Always use pot holders and direct the release of steam away from yourself.

To determine if the pudding is done, remove the mold and insert a sharp knife or wooden pick in the center of the pudding. The blade or pick should come out cleanly when the pudding is done.

Allow the pudding to stand, uncovered, for 10-15 minutes in the mold. The pudding should shrink away from the sides of the mold during this time; however, you may need to run a knife carefully around the inside edges of the mold to loosen it completely.

Place an inverted plate over the mold, and, grasping the mold and the plate together, turn them over. The pudding should slide out easily. Serve the steamed pudding hot at the table.

If you wish to freeze the pudding for later use, allow the pudding to cool to room temperature. Then wrap it in heavy foil or double thicknesses of plastic wrap, and seal it in a large self-sealing freezer bag or tie a plastic freezer bag securely with twister seals. To reheat frozen steamed puddings, defrost and steam in the original mold or wrapped in buttered or oiled foil for one to two hours.

Sauces are a natural complement to many puddings, and many sauces are interchangeable and create a very unique but satisfying variation. You may interchange fruit sauces with a wide variety of both fruit and cream puddings. Be imaginative about this. Also, interchange fruits and nuts in fruit pudding recipes to fit your particular tastes.

Incorporating apples and cranberries, this royal dessert is prepared in a pudding mold and is served inverted from the mold.

APPLE-CRANBERRY CROWN PUDDING

SERVES 6-8

1 cup self-rising flour

¼ teaspoon salt

½ cup shredded suet

5 to 7 tablespoons ice water

1½ pounds Granny Smith apples, peeled,
  cored, sliced

1 cup chopped cranberries

¼ cup sugar

½ teaspoon cinnamon

First, make the pastry. Use a food processor fitted with steel blade. Combine flour and salt. Mix in suet. Pour water slowly through the feed tube with the machine running until a dough is formed. Gather dough and roll out on lightly floured board into a circle large enough to cover the bowl of the mold. Carefully pat the crust into a 1½-quart pudding bowl, covering the inside of the bowl.

Toss apples with cranberries, sugar, and cinnamon. Arrange fruit, filling in bowl. Bring pastry edges over apples. Cover with greased aluminum foil and tie securely with string.

Set on a rack in a steamer or large saucepan. Pour water halfway up the sides of bowl. Cook over high heat until water boils. Reduce heat to simmer and cover. Steam pudding 2½-2¾ hours. Check pan after 45 minutes, adding more water as necessary.

To unmold, remove foil, let stand 5 minutes. Invert onto a serving plate. Serve warm.

APPLESAUCE PUDDING WITH BUTTERSCOTCH SAUCE

SERVES 6

¼ cup butter or margarine

½ cup firmly packed light brown sugar

1 egg

1 egg white

1¼ cups unbleached all-purpose flour

1 cup graham cracker crumbs

1 teaspoon baking powder

½ teaspoon baking soda

½ cup buttermilk

1¼ cups applesauce

1 cup ground pecans

1 teaspoon ground cinnamon

½ teaspoon ground allspice, ground
    ginger

BUTTERSCOTCH SAUCE

½ cup firmly packed dark brown sugar

2 tablespoons cornstarch

¼ cup butter or margarine, cut in ½-inch
    pieces

½ cup hot water

½ cup milk

¾ teaspoon vanilla

Cream butter and sugar until light. Beat in egg and egg white. Mix in flour, graham cracker crumbs, baking powder, and baking soda.

Blend in buttermilk, applesauce, pecans, and spices.

Spoon batter into a well-greased 1½-quart pudding mold. Cover with greased aluminum foil or a cloth and tie securely with string.

Set on a rack in steamer or large saucepan. Pour water halfway up the sides of mold. Cook over high heat until water boils. Reduce heat to simmer and cover. Steam pudding about 1½ hours. Check pan after 45 minutes, adding more water as necessary.

While pudding is steaming, prepare sauce. Stir sugar and cornstarch together in a saucepan. Add butter, hot water, and milk, then simmer for 7-8 minutes, or until golden in color and slightly thickened. Remove from heat, stir in vanilla. Set aside until needed.

To unmold pudding, run a knife along the inside edge of mold and invert onto serving dish. Serve pudding sliced *over* a pool of Butterscotch Sauce.

APRICOT PUDDING WITH ORANGE CURD

SERVES 6-8

½ cup vegetable shortening

½ cup sugar

2 eggs

1 egg white

2 cups unbleached all-purpose flour

¾ teaspoon baking powder

¾ teaspoon baking soda

¾ cup orange juice

⅓ cup candied orange peel

1½ cups chopped, dried apricots

½ cup golden raisins

½ cup ground hazelnuts

½ teaspoon ground cardamom

ORANGE CURD

¾ cup orange juice

½-¾ cup sugar

2 eggs

1 egg yolk

5 tablespoons butter or margarine, at room
temperature, cut into small pieces

2 tablespoons grated orange peel

Cream shortening and sugar until light. Beat in eggs and egg white. Mix in flour, baking powder, baking soda, and orange juice. Add candied orange peel, apricots, raisins, hazelnuts, and cardamom.

Spoon batter into a greased 1½-quart pudding mold. Cover with greased aluminum foil or a cloth and tie securely with string.

Set on a rack in a steamer or large saucepan. Pour water halfway up the sides of bowl. Cook over high heat until water boils. Reduce heat to simmer, cover. Steam pudding about 1½ hours. Check pan after 45 minutes, adding more water as necessary.

While pudding is steaming, prepare orange curd. Grate 2 tablespoons of peel from the oranges. Set aside.

Squeeze the juice from the oranges and strain into the top of a double boiler over simmering water. Whisk in sugar and eggs. Cook orange mixture, whisking almost constantly until mixture thickens.

Remove orange mixture from heat. Whisk in butter and orange peel. Spoon orange curd into a bowl. Cover and refrigerate until needed.

To unmold pudding, run a knife along inside edge of mold and invert onto serving dish. Serve pudding hot with orange curd.

This recipe is an adaptation of our family's favorite. Left over cake can be made into crumbs by discarding the frosting and crumbling the cake into a plastic bag. Seal the bag securely and freeze crumbs until needed.

BANANA PUDDING

SERVES 6

5 tablespoons butter or margarine

¾ cup firmly packed light brown sugar

2 eggs

3 large ripe bananas

¾ cup vanilla low-fat yogurt

2 cups unbleached all-purpose flour

½ cup cake crumbs

1 teaspoon baking powder

1 teaspoon baking soda

½ teaspoon salt

½ teaspoon ground cinnamon

¼ teaspoon ground nutmeg

1 cup ground walnuts

½ cup dried, chopped pineapple

Cream butter and sugar until light. Beat in eggs and bananas. Blend in yogurt. Mix in flour, cake crumbs, baking powder, and baking soda. Add salt, cinnamon, nutmeg, walnuts, and pineapple.

Spoon batter into a greased 1½-quart or loaf-pan pudding mold. Cover with greased aluminum foil or a cloth and tie securely with string.

Set on a rack in steamer or large saucepan. Pour water halfway up the sides of bowl. Cook over high heat until water boils. Reduce heat to simmer and cover. Steam pudding about 1½ hours. Check pan after 45 minutes, adding more water as necessary.

Let pudding stand 5 minutes. To unmold, run a knife around the inside edge of pudding. Invert pudding onto serving dish and serve hot.

CARROT PUDDING WITH HARD SAUCE

SERVES 6-8

4 tablespoons butter, margarine, or vegetable
   shortening
¾ cup firmly packed light brown sugar
3 eggs
¾ cup unbleached all-purpose flour
1½ cups fine bread crumbs
½ cup chopped pecans
1 teaspoon baking soda
1½ teaspoons ground cinnamon
¼ teaspoon nutmeg
¼ teaspoon ground cloves
¼ teaspoon ground allspice
¼ teaspoon salt
1¼ cups grated carrots

RUM HARD SAUCE

12 tablespoons butter at room temperature
1½ cups confectioner's sugar
⅛ teaspoon salt
3 tablespoons dark rum

Cream the 4 tablespoons butter or shortening and brown sugar until light. Blend in eggs. Add the flour, bread crumbs, pecans, and baking soda. Mix in spices, salt, and carrots.

Spoon batter into a greased 1½-quart pudding mold. Cover with buttered aluminum foil or a cloth. Tie securely with string.

Set pudding on a rack in a steamer or large saucepan. Pour water halfway up the sides of bowl.

Cook over high heat until water boils. Reduce heat to simmer and cover. Steam pudding 1½ hours. Check pan after 45 minutes, adding more water as necessary.

While pudding is steaming, prepare sauce. Cut the butter into ½-inch cubes and place in a bowl. Cream the butter and sugar until light. Mix in salt and rum. Spoon into a crock. Bring to room temperature before serving.

To unmold pudding, let pudding cool 5 minutes. Run a knife around the inside edge of bowl. Invert pudding on dish and serve immediately with sauce.

ONE-CUP
CURRANT PUDDING

SERVES 8

1 cup shredded suet

1 cup sugar

1 cup unbleached all-purpose flour

1 cup bread crumbs

1 teaspoon baking soda

1 cup milk, scalded and cooled

1 cup currants

1 cup currant jam

STRAWBERRY SAUCE

3 cups washed, sliced strawberries

½ cup sugar

3 tablespoons freshly squeezed orange juice

Mix suet and sugar together. Blend in flour and bread crumbs. Add baking soda to cool milk and blend into batter. Add currants and jam.

Spoon into a greased 1½-quart pudding bowl. Cover with greased aluminum foil or a cloth and tie securely with string.

Set on a rack in a steamer or large saucepan. Pour water halfway up the sides of bowl. Cook over high heat until water boils. Reduce heat to simmer and cover. Steam pudding about 2½ hours. Check pan after 45 minutes, adding more water as necessary.

While pudding is cooking, prepare strawberries. Combine all Strawberry Sauce ingredients in a saucepan and simmer 5 minutes, stirring often.

SPOTTED DOG PUDDING

SERVES 6

½ cup butter or margarine

3 tablespoons sugar

2 eggs

¼ teaspoon salt

1½ cups unbleached all-purpose flour

1 teaspoon baking powder

½ cup milk

¾ cup currants

Cream butter and sugar until light. Mix in eggs. Add salt, flour, and baking powder. Add milk and currants.

Spoon batter into a greased 1½-quart pudding mold. Cover with greased aluminum foil or a cloth and tie securely with string.

Set pudding on a rack in steamer or large saucepan. Pour water halfway up the sides of bowl. Cook over high heat until water boils. Reduce heat to simmer and cover. Steam pudding about 1½ hours. Check pan after 45 minutes, adding more water as necessary.

To unmold pudding, run a knife around the inside edge of bowl. Invert pudding on dish. Serve with brown sugar.

DATE AND PECAN PUDDING

SERVES 6-8

1¼ cup chopped dates

¾ cup boiling water

½ cup vegetable shortening or margarine

½ cup sugar

2 eggs

½ cup molasses

2 cups unbleached all-purpose flour

1 teaspoon baking powder

1 teaspoon baking soda

1 teaspoon ground cinnamon

½ teaspoon salt

½ teaspoon ground ginger

¼ teaspoon ground nutmeg

1 teaspoon vanilla

~~1 cup chopped pecans~~

VANILLA SAUCE

6 tablespoons butter or margarine at room
    temperature, cut into ½ inch pieces

1 cup sugar

1¼ teaspoons vanilla

2 tablespoons sherry

1 pint half-and-half or milk

Cover dates with water and set aside.

Cream shortening or margarine and sugar until light. Beat in eggs and molasses. Mix in flour, baking powder, baking soda, cinnamon,

---

salt, ginger, nutmeg, and vanilla. Blend in dates, including liquid, and nuts.

Spoon batter into a greased 1½-quart mold. Cover with greased aluminum foil or a cloth. Tie securely with string.

Set on a rack in a steamer or large saucepan. Pour water halfway up sides of bowl. Cook over high heat until water boils. Reduce heat to simmer and cover. Steam pudding 1½-2 hours. Check pan after 45 minutes, adding more water as necessary.

While pudding is steaming, prepare sauce. Cream butter and sugar until light. Mix in vanilla and sherry. Blend in half-and-half or milk. Pour into bowl and refrigerate until needed. Stir before serving.

Let pudding cool 5 minutes. To unmold, run a knife around the inside of bowl. Invert onto dish. Serve pudding hot with Vanilla Sauce.

FIGGY PUDDING

SERVES 6-8

½ pound dried figs

5 tablespoons butter, margarine, or vegetable
shortening

½ cup sugar

2 eggs

1 large tart apple, peeled, cored, and grated

1 teaspoon baking powder

¼ teaspoon salt

¼ teaspoon nutmeg

2 cups fine bread crumbs

1 cup milk

Chop figs, set aside. Cream butter or margarine with sugar. Blend in eggs, apple, baking powder, nutmeg, and salt. Mix in crumbs, figs, and milk. Spoon batter into a greased 1½-quart pudding mold. Cover with greased aluminum foil or a cloth and tie securely with string.

Set mold on a rack in a steamer or large saucepan. Pour water halfway up the side of the bowl. Cook over high heat until water boils. Reduce heat to simmer and cover. Steam pudding 1½ hours. Check pan after 45 minutes, adding more water as necessary.

To unmold pudding, run a knife around the inside edge of bowl. Invert pudding on dish and serve hot with whipped cream.

GINGERBREAD PUDDING

SERVES 8-10

5 tablespoons butter, margarine, or vegetable
  shortening

½ cup firmly packed light brown sugar

½ cup molasses

1 egg

2 egg whites

2 cups unbleached all-purpose flour

1 teaspoon baking soda

½ teaspoon baking powder

½ cup plain non-fat yogurt

1 cup ground walnuts

½ cup sultana raisins

LEMON CURD

½ cup freshly squeezed lemon juice

¾ cup sugar

2 eggs

1 egg yolk

4 tablespoons butter or margarine at room
  temperature, cut into small pieces

Cream butter and sugar until light. Add molasses. Beat in egg and egg whites. Stir in flour, baking soda, and baking powder. Blend in yogurt and nuts.

Spread sultana raisins over the bottom of a greased 1½-quart pudding mold. Spoon batter over sultanas in pan. Cover with greased aluminum foil or a cloth and tie securely with string.

Set pudding on rack in steamer or large saucepan. Pour water halfway up sides of mold. Cook over high heat until water boils.

Reduce heat to simmer and cover. Steam pudding 1½ hours. Check pan after 45 minutes, adding more water as necessary.

While pudding is steaming, prepare Lemon Curd.

Squeeze the juice from the lemons and strain into the top of a double boiler over simmering water. Whisk in sugar and eggs. Cook lemon mixture, whisking almost constantly until mixture thickens.

Remove lemon mixture from heat. Whisk in butter. Spoon lemon curd into a bowl. Cover and refrigerate until needed. Makes about 1 cup.

To unmold pudding, run a knife around the inside edge of bowl. Invert pudding on dish. Serve hot Gingerbread Pudding with Lemon Curd Sauce.

Also good chilled, sliced, and fried. An old New England recipe.

STEAMED HASTY PUDDING

SERVES 6

½ teaspoon salt

½ teaspoon ground cinnamon

3 cups water

½ cup cornmeal

Maple syrup

Mix salt and cinnamon with 3 cups of water in a saucepan. Bring to a full boil over medium heat. Whisk in the cornmeal, crushing out any lumps. Continue boiling for 1 minute. Cover.

Set covered pan in a steamer or large saucepan on a rack over boiling water and cover steamer. Steam 25 minutes. Uncover and bring pudding to table hot. Serve with maple syrup.

From Maggie Hildebrandt's mother's handwritten cookbook. Circa 1910.

HUNT PUDDING

SERVES 6-8

4 tablespoons butter or margarine at room
   temperature

¼ cup sugar

2 eggs

2 cups unbleached all-purpose flour

1 teaspoon baking soda

¼ teaspoon salt

1 teaspoon vanilla

1 cup buttermilk

1 cup raspberry jam

LEMON SAUCE

½ cup sugar

1¼ tablespoons cornstarch

1 cup water

2 teaspoons grated lemon zest

4 tablespoons lemon juice

4 tablespoons butter or margarine at room
   temperature

Cream butter or margarine with sugar until light. Beat in eggs. Mix in flour, baking soda, and salt. Mix in vanilla, buttermilk, and jam.

Spoon batter into a greased 1½-quart pudding mold. Cover with greased aluminum foil or a cloth. Tie securely with string.

Set pudding mold on a rack in a steamer or large saucepan. Pour water halfway up the sides of the bowl.

Cook over high heat until water boils. Reduce heat to simmer and cover. Steam pudding 1½ hours. Check pan after 45 minutes, adding more water as necessary.

While pudding is steaming, prepare sauce. Combine sugar and cornstarch in a saucepan. Mix in water. Bring mixture to a boil over medium heat. Simmer for 10 minutes, stirring often. Mix in zest, juice, and butter. Stir to combine. Serve warm or hot.

Let pudding cool 5 minutes. To unmold pudding, run a knife around the inside of bowl. Invert onto dish. Serve pudding hot with Lemon Sauce.

LEMON PUDDING

SERVES 6

5 tablespoons butter or margarine

¾ cup sugar

3 eggs

2 cups unbleached all-purpose flour

1 teaspoon baking powder

1 teaspoon baking soda

¼ teaspoon salt

5 tablespoons freshly squeezed lemon juice

2 tablespoons grated lemon peel

APRICOT GLAZE

3 tablespoons apricot jam

1 tablespoon water

Cream butter or margarine with sugar until light. Beat in eggs. Combine separately the flour, baking powder, baking soda, and salt, and add the dry ingredients to the creamed mixture. Blend in lemon juice and peel.

Spoon batter into a greased 1½-quart pudding mold. Cover with greased aluminum foil or a cloth and tie securely with string.

Set pudding on a rack in a steamer or large saucepan. Pour water halfway up the sides of bowl. Cook over high heat until water boils. Reduce heat to simmer and cover. Steam pudding about 1½ hours. Check pan after 45 minutes, adding more water as necessary.

While pudding is steaming, mix jam with water. Heat in small saucepan, stirring often until jam melts. Set aside.

To unmold pudding, run a knife around the inside edge of bowl. Invert pudding on dish. Pour glaze over pudding. Serve immediately.

MARMALADE PUDDING WITH LEMON SAUCE

SERVES 6-8

4 tablespoons margarine or butter

¼ cup sugar

2 eggs

2 cups unbleached all-purpose flour

2 teaspoons baking powder

¼ teaspoon salt

½ cup milk

¾ cup orange marmalade

LEMON SAUCE II

2 tablespoons cornstarch

⅓ cup sugar

⅓ cup freshly squeezed lemon juice

1¼ cups water

3 tablespoons butter or margarine

Cream butter or margarine and sugar together until light. Blend in eggs. Combine flour, baking powder, and salt in a separate bowl. Add the dry ingredients to the creamed mixture alternately with the milk.

Melt the orange marmalade with 1 tablespoon of water.

Pour the marmalade into a well-greased 1½-quart pudding mold. Tip mold so that marmalade covers some of the sides of the mold. Spoon batter into the mold. Cover with greased aluminum foil or a cloth and tie securely with string.

Set on a rack in a steamer or large saucepan. Pour water halfway up the sides of bowl. Cook over high heat until water boils. Reduce heat to simmer, cover, and continue cooking 1½ hours. Check water after 45 minutes, adding more water as necessary.

While pudding is steaming, prepare sauce. Mix cornstarch with sugar in a bowl. Blend in juice and water. Pour mixture into a small saucepan and cook over medium heat, stirring often, until mixture is clear and slightly thickened. Beat in butter. Serve warm or cold.

To unmold pudding, run a knife around the inside edge of bowl. Invert pudding onto dish and serve hot with Lemon Sauce.

Muesli is a dry cereal, a combination of fruit, nut and grains. It originated in Europe but now is popular in America and available in supermarkets in the cereal section.

MUESLI PUDDING

SERVES 6

5 tablespoons butter or margarine

¾ cup light brown sugar

2 eggs

¾ cup smooth peanut butter

1¼ cup Muesli

1 cup unbleached all-purpose flour

1 teaspoon baking powder

½ teaspoon baking soda

1 cup non-fat vanilla yogurt

½ teaspoon salt

½ teaspoon ground cinnamon

1 cup chopped peanuts

½ cup golden raisins

Cream butter and sugar until light. Blend in eggs and peanut butter. Mix in Muesli, flour, baking powder, and baking soda. Add yogurt, salt, cinnamon, peanuts, and raisins.

Spoon batter into a well-greased 1½-quart pudding mold. Cover with greased aluminum foil or a cloth and tie securely with string.

Set on a rack in a steamer or large saucepan. Pour water halfway up the sides of bowl. Cook over high heat until water boils. Reduce heat to simmer and cover. Steam pudding about 1½ hours. Check pan after 45 minutes, adding more water as necessary.

Let pudding rest 5 minutes. To unmold, run a knife around the inside edge of bowl. Invert pudding on dish and serve immediately. Good with vanilla yogurt.

STEAMED
HOLIDAY PUDDINGS

One of the great moments at the holiday table is when the hostess presents the heritage culinary treat of a steaming, glowing holiday pudding with sauce. Steamed pudding is easy to prepare for holiday time as it can be made weeks in advance and then be microwaved or resteamed to bring the pudding to its full glory. The pudding is brought to room temperature and resteamed for one hour, or until hot, in its original mold. If it is to be microwaved, it is set on a non-metallic plate and covered loosely with plastic wrap and microwaved for a few minutes until the pudding is steaming hot.

For some, the sight of the holiday pudding, especially at Christmas and Thanksgiving, brings up thoughts of holidays past and gatherings of family and sharing. For others, the pudding is a wonderful alternative to a conventional dessert and a new creative experience for the hostess or host looking for a new idea.

This is an ideal Thanksgiving Day dessert, an alternative to pumpkin pie. I have adapted this recipe from my own recipe for shortbread. I have used canned pumpkin for convenience, but you may certainly use fresh pumpkin. The crystallized ginger gives this dessert a sparkle and a zest that is wonderful.

PUMPKIN PUDDING WITH CUSTARD SAUCE

SERVES 6-8

6 tablespoons butter or margarine

½ cup firmly packed light brown sugar

4 eggs

¼ cup molasses

3 tablespoons dark rum or brandy

1 can (16 ounces) pumpkin purée

¾ cup milk

½ cup chopped crystallized ginger

½ cup chopped walnuts

1½ cups unbleached all-purpose flour

1 teaspoon baking powder

1 teaspoon baking soda

¾ cup gingersnap crumbs

1 teaspoon ground cinnamon

½ teaspoon salt

½ teaspoon pumpkin pie spice

CUSTARD SAUCE

4 egg yolks

¼ cup sugar

3 tablespoons unbleached all-purpose flour

2 cups milk, scalded

2 tablespoons rum

Cream butter or margarine with sugar until light. Blend in eggs, molasses, rum, pumpkin purée, and milk. Mix in ginger and nuts. Add flour, baking powder, baking soda, and crumbs. Mix in spices.

Spoon batter into a buttered 1½-quart pudding mold. Cover with greased aluminum foil or a cloth. Tie securely with a string.

Set pudding on a rack in a steamer or large saucepan. Pour water halfway up the sides of bowl.

Cook over high heat until water boils. Reduce heat to simmer and cover. Steam pudding 1½-2 hours. Check pan after 45 minutes, adding more water as necessary.

While pudding is steaming, prepare sauce. Whisk together the yolks, sugar, and flour. Whisk in milk in a slow, steady stream.

Pour sauce into top of double boiler over simmering water. Cook, stirring constantly until sauce thickens. Remove from heat and stir in rum. Cool.

Let pudding cool 5 minutes. To unmold, run a knife around the inside edge of bowl and invert onto serving dish.

Serve Pumpkin Pudding hot with Custard Sauce.

BLACK FIG
CHRISTMAS PUDDING

½ cup chopped candied fruit

1½ cups chopped black figs

⅓ cup ground walnuts

2 cups unbleached all-purpose flour, divided

⅓ cup suet or vegetable shortening

¼ cup molasses

1 egg

2 egg whites

¾ teaspoon baking soda

1 teaspoon baking powder

1 teaspoon ground cinnamon

½ teaspoon ground ginger

½ teaspoon salt

¼ teaspoon ground cloves

½ cup milk

¼ cup brandy

Custard Sauce (page 30) with 2 tablespoons
    brandy

Sprinkle fruits and nuts with ¼ cup of the flour. Set aside.

Cream shortening with molasses. Beat in egg and egg whites. Stir in remaining flour, baking soda, baking powder, and spices. Mix in milk, fruit, and brandy.

Spoon batter into a buttered 1½-quart mold. Cover with greased aluminum foil or a cloth and tie securely with string.

Set pudding on a rack in steamer or large saucepan. Pour water halfway up the sides of bowl. Cook over high heat until water boils. Reduce heat to simmer and cover. Steam pudding about 1½ hours. Check pan after 45 minutes, adding more water as necessary.

While pudding is steaming, prepare Custard Sauce according to recipe, using brandy instead of the rum. Cool.

To unmold pudding, run a knife around the inside edge of bowl. Invert pudding on dish. Serve Christmas Pudding hot with brandy Custard Sauce and garnish. Also good with whipped cream.

Plum pudding is a dessert that is as much associated with the Christmas dinner as anything could be. The words plum pudding *evoke a perfect sense of Christmas merriment and the true harmony, peace, and joy that this holiday connotes. The shadow of Charles Dickens and the angelic smile of Tiny Tim stand witness to the entry of the plum pudding to the Christmas dinner table. In this recipe, I have used both a traditional single mold and ½ cup molds so that each family member or guest may glory in his own individual plum pudding. These puddings have long been immortalized in children's rhymes.*

INDIVIDUAL PLUM PUDDINGS

SERVES 10-12

¾ cup chopped, assorted candied fruit

¾ cup currants

½ cup raisins

1¼ cups stewed pitted prunes

½ cup chopped walnuts

½ cup candied citron

1 cup candied cherries

¼ cup sherry or brandy

5 tablespoons butter at room temperature

¼ cup firmly packed light brown sugar

3 eggs

¼ cup molasses

⅔ cup unbleached all-purpose flour

⅔ cup fine bread crumbs

1 teaspoon baking powder

¾ teaspoon ground cinnamon

¼ teaspoon ground cloves

¼ teaspoon ground nutmeg

¼ teaspoon ground ginger

¼ teaspoon salt

¼ cup milk

BRANDY HARD SAUCE

¾ cup butter or margarine at room
   temperature
1½ cups confectioner's sugar
4 tablespoons brandy

Toss all fruits and walnuts with brandy. Let stand 15 minutes and then stir.

Cream butter and sugar until light. Beat in eggs and molasses. Mix in flour, crumbs, baking powder, and spices. Add marinating fruits and milk.

Spoon butter into a greased 7-cup mold or twelve ½-cup individual molds. Cover with greased aluminum foil. Tie securely with string.

Set mold on a rack in a steamer or large saucepan. Pour water halfway up the sides of bowl. Cook on high heat until water begins to boil. Reduce heat to simmer and cover. Steam 3 hours. Check occasionally, adding more water as necessary.

Cool 10 minutes. To unmold pudding, run a knife around the inside edge of bowl. Invert pudding onto a dish. To store, cool completely, cover in three layers of brandy-soaked cheesecloth and tightly wrapped in foil. Every 3 or 4 days, unwrap pudding and drizzle cloth with brandy. Refrigerate for 2 months if necessary.

Resteam pudding for 45 minutes before serving. Set on serving dish and garnish.

To make Brandy Hard Sauce, cream butter and sugar until light. Mix in brandy. Spoon into a crock, cover, and refrigerate until needed. Remove from refrigerator 1 hour before serving.

To flame pudding, heat ⅓ cup brandy in small pan. Light the brandy and drizzle over pudding. Serve with Brandy Hard Sauce when flame is extinguished.

BAKED PUDDINGS

Baked puddings are irresistible. They are easy and relatively inexpensive to make. They are good for that special occasion like a graduation or a birthday or for a family meal. In this chapter we have included such old favorites as Berry Cottage Pudding, Cracker Pudding, and Indian Pudding and such new puddings as Raisin Bread Pudding with Whiskey Sauce and Almond Noodle Pudding.

APPLE AND ALMOND NOODLE PUDDING

SERVES 10-12

1 pound medium-width noodles, cooked
   according to package directions

¾ cup sliced almonds

¾ cup golden raisins

4 Golden Delicious apples, peeled and diced

4 eggs, separated

1 egg white

1 cup milk

1 tablespoon ground cinnamon

3 tablespoons melted butter or margarine

Drain noodles and place in a deep bowl. Mix in almonds, raisins, and apples. Blend in egg yolks. Beat egg whites until stiff. Fold whites into noodle mixture. Gently mix in milk, cinnamon, and butter.

Spoon into greased 9 x 13-inch ovenproof dish and bake at 350°F. for 1 hour or until pudding tests done by inserting a cake tester and having it come out of pudding dry. Cool. Cut in squares and serve warm or cold.

I am one of the lucky ones who grew up in a family with a grandmother. An early memory is of my grandmother saving a few pieces of leftover bread each week and then my watching her create her special pudding. Each week the bread pudding would be different, based on the fruit that was available – apricots or apples or berries or dried fruits. But whatever the magic combination was, it is her bread pudding that I remember so fondly.

APRICOT CUSTARD BREAD PUDDING

SERVES 6-8

6 slices white bread, crusts removed (egg bread or hard rolls make the best puddings)

3 cups milk, scalded and cooled

5 eggs

½ cup sugar

1 teaspoon vanilla

1½ cups drained, pitted, and chopped apricots (canned, dried, or fresh)

2 tablespoons butter or margarine, cut in small pieces

½ teaspoon ground cinnamon

Tear the bread into 1-inch pieces and place in a mixing bowl. Add the cooled milk and let stand for 10 minutes. Meanwhile beat the eggs and sugar until light. Mix in vanilla, apricots, butter, and cinnamon.

Pour the pudding into a greased 2-quart baking bowl or pan. (I use my pudding mold.) Set the bowl in a larger baking pan and fill halfway with hot water. Bake the pudding in a 350°F. oven for 1¼ hours or until the pudding tests done. Stir pudding once or twice during the first 30 minutes of baking. To test pudding insert a knife; if it comes out clean the pudding is done. Cool pudding. It is good served warm or cold.

BERRY
COTTAGE PUDDING

1 cup hulled strawberries or blueberries

4 tablespoons butter or margarine

¾ cup sugar

1 egg

½ cup milk

1½ cups unbleached all-purpose flour

2 teaspoons baking powder

½ cup firmly packed light brown sugar

2 teaspoons unbleached all-purpose flour

4 tablespoons butter or margarine at room
   temperature, cut into small pieces

½ teaspoon ground cinnamon

Pick over berries, discarding any bruised berries. Wash the fruit and drain on paper towels. Set aside.

Cream butter and sugar together until light. Add egg and milk. Mix in 1½ cups flour and baking powder. Gently fold in fruit.

Ladle batter into a greased 9 x 9-inch baking pan. Combine brown sugar, remaining flour, butter, and cinnamon and sprinkle over pudding. Bake in a 350°F. oven for 45-55 minutes or until pudding tests done.

Spoon warm pudding into dessert dishes. Good with sweetened strawberries or strawberry yogurt.

Bird's nest puddings were prepared by having either sliced apples or whole apples in the center of the pudding, which gives the appearance of a bird's nest.

BIRD'S NEST PUDDING WITH WHOLE APPLES

SERVES 6

2 cups sugar

1 cup water

6 medium apples, whole but cored
  and peeled

2 cups half-and-half

3 eggs, beaten

¼ cup sugar

2 teaspoons vanilla

Blend 2 cups sugar and water in a saucepan. Cook over medium heat until sugar is dissolved. Slide apples into the syrup. Cover and simmer for 7 minutes, turning once or twice.

Remove apples from syrup and arrange in a greased 1-quart shallow baking dish.

Scald half-and-half. Cool. Add eggs slowly. Mix in ¼ cup sugar and vanilla. Pour mixture around apples. Set dish in a roaster or other larger dish. Fill with hot water halfway up sides of dish.

Bake pudding in 325°F. oven for 45-55 minutes or until a knife inserted in the center of custard comes out clean.

BIRD'S NEST PUDDING WITH SLICED APPLES

SERVES 6

5 large apples, peeled, sliced

1 egg

¾ cup milk

½ cup sugar

½ teaspoon salt

1 teaspoon baking powder

1 cup unbleached all-purpose flour

2 tablespoons butter or margarine, melted

Arrange the apples evenly in a greased pie plate. Set aside.

Mix together the egg, milk, sugar, salt, baking powder, flour, and butter.

Gently pour batter over the apples. Bake pudding at 350° F. for 25 minutes.

Serve pudding hot or warm.

BREAD PUDDING WITH MERINGUE

SERVES 6

3½ cups day-old bread with crust discarded

3 cups milk, scalded

4 eggs, separated

¾ cup sugar, divided

1 teaspoon grated lemon peel

½ cup candied lemon or orange peel, chopped

½ teaspoon ground cinnamon

1½ teaspoons vanilla

Tear bread into 1-inch pieces and set in a mixing bowl. Stir in milk and let stand 10-15 minutes. Beat egg yolks and mix with ½ cup of sugar, lemon peel, candied lemon peel, cinnamon, and vanilla. Stir egg mixture into bread and milk.

Pour bread pudding into 2-quart baking dish. Set in a larger shallow pan. Fill with hot water to halfway up sides of baking dish. Bake at 325°F. for 1¼ hours or until pudding tests done.

Beat egg whites until soft peaks form. Sprinkle with remaining sugar. Continue beating until stiff peaks form. Spread meringue over bread pudding. Bake pudding 10 minutes more or until meringue is slightly brown. Remove from oven. Serve warm or cold.

What book on puddings would be complete without this version of bread pudding? The following is my rendition of a very popular pudding.

BREAD PUDDING
WITH WHISKEY SAUCE

SERVES 6

3 cups bread (crust discarded) or rolls torn
　　into small pieces
1 quart milk, scalded
5 eggs
1 cup sugar
1½-2 teaspoons vanilla
1¼ cups dark raisins
3 tablespoons butter or margarine, cut in
　　small pieces
1 cup grated apples

WHISKEY SAUCE

8 tablespoons butter
1 cup sugar
1 egg
2 tablespoons whiskey or to taste

Place bread in a deep mixing bowl. Stir in milk. Let stand for 15 minutes. Meanwhile beat the eggs with sugar until light. Blend in vanilla, raisins, butter, and apples. Stir egg mixture into bread and milk.

Pour bread pudding into a 2-quart shallow baking dish. Bake at 350°F. for 45-55 minutes or until the pudding tests done. A knife inserted in the center of the pudding will come out clean. Cool.

While pudding is cooling, prepare sauce. Beat the butter and sugar until light. Spoon into the top of a double boiler over simmering water. Whisk in the egg and continue cooking, whisking almost constantly until sauce thickens slightly. Remove sauce from heat, cool. When sauce has cooled stir in whiskey.

Serve pudding warm or cool, covered with sauce.

CRACKER PUDDING

SERVES 6

5 eggs, separated
¾ cup sugar
⅛ teaspoon salt
¾ cup cracker crumbs
2½ cups milk, scalded and cooled
¼ cup butter or margarine, melted
2 teaspoons vanilla, divided
¼ cup sugar

Beat the egg yolks with ¾ cup sugar and salt until light. Mix in crumbs and milk. Add butter and stir in 1 teaspoon of the vanilla.

Ladle pudding into a 2-quart baking dish. Bake the pudding in a 350°F. oven for 45-60 minutes or until the pudding tests done.

While the pudding is baking, prepare meringue. Beat the egg whites until soft peaks form. Sprinkle remaining sugar over the egg whites and incorporate. Blend in the remaining vanilla.

Mound meringue over top and sides of slightly cooled pudding to seal the pudding. Bake again in a 350°F. oven for about 5 to 6 minutes or until the tips of meringue are a golden brown. Cool.

Eve's Pudding

6 tablespoons butter or margarine

1 cup sugar

3 eggs

1 tablespoon grated lemon peel

1 teaspoon vanilla

1 cup bread crumbs

4 large Granny Smith apples, peeled, cored,
and sliced thin

Beat butter and sugar until light. Blend in eggs, peel, vanilla, and bread crumbs. Arrange apple slices in a greased 9-inch pie plate. Pour egg mixture over the apples.

Bake in a 375°F. oven for 30 minutes or until apples are tender.

GRAPE-NUTS PUDDING

SERVES 6

1½ cups Grape-Nuts, soaked in ½ cup
   boiling water for 10 minutes
2 cups milk
½ cup sugar
½ teaspoon ground cinnamon
⅛ teaspoon salt
3 eggs

Add milk, sugar, cinnamon, and salt to Grape-Nuts mixture. Beat eggs until light. Blend into pudding mixture.

Pour pudding into a 1½-quart ovenproof mold. Bake in a 325°F. oven for 45 minutes or until a knife inserted in the center of pudding comes out clean. Cool pudding on a rack.

Spoon pudding into individual dishes and serve cold with milk or cream.

INDIAN PUDDING
WITH RAISINS

SERVES 6

3 cups milk

⅔ cup molasses

⅓ cup cornmeal

¼ cup butter or margarine

¾ cup golden raisins

½ teaspoon ground ginger

½ teaspoon ground cinnamon

¼ teaspoon ground nutmeg

¼ teaspoon salt

2 eggs, slightly beaten

1 cup milk

Scald 3 cups milk. Stir in molasses and cornmeal. Bring milk mixture to a boil over medium heat. Reduce heat to a simmer and cook about 18 to 20 minutes, stirring occasionally.

Remove pan from heat and cool. Stir in butter or margarine, raisins, ginger, cinnamon, nutmeg, salt, and eggs. Pour pudding into a 2-quart baking dish.

Bake pudding in a 350°F. oven for 1¼-1½ hours or until the pudding tests done. After 20 minutes of baking, pour remaining cup of milk over top of pudding.

Serve pudding hot with vanilla ice cream.

INDIAN PUDDING II

SERVES 6

3½ cups milk

¼ cup cornmeal

¼ cup light brown sugar

5 eggs

¼ cup molasses

½ teaspoon ground cinnamon

¼ teaspoon ground nutmeg

Scald milk. Stir in cornmeal and sugar. Cool. Beat eggs with molasses and spices. Stir egg mixture into cooled milk.

Pour pudding into a 2-quart ovenproof dish and set in a larger baking pan. Fill the baking pan with hot water halfway up the sides of pudding dish.

Bake in a 400°F. oven for 1½-1¾ hours or until a knife inserted in center comes out dry.

Serve hot with vanilla ice cream or whipped cream.

ORANGE
SPONGE PUDDING

SERVES 4

3 egg yolks

¾ cup sugar

⅓ cup freshly squeezed orange juice

1 tablespoon grated orange peel

2 tablespoons cornstarch

1½ cups milk, scalded and cooled

Beat egg yolks and sugar until light. Mix in juice, orange peel, cornstarch, and milk.

Pour pudding into a 1-quart baking dish. Set in a slightly larger pan and add hot water halfway up the sides of the baking pan. Bake in a 350°F. oven for 45 minutes or until the pudding tests done. Cool. Spoon the pudding into individual dishes.

RAISIN BREAD PUDDING

SERVES 6

¼ cup sherry

1¼ cups golden raisins

4 cups day-old white or egg bread, trimmed,
   buttered, and cubed

5 eggs, beaten

¼ cup sugar

3 cups milk, scalded and cooled

¼ teaspoon ground nutmeg

½ teaspoon ground cinnamon

1 teaspoon vanilla

Pour sherry over the raisins in a shallow bowl and let stand for 20 minutes.

Meanwhile arrange the bread cubes in a 2-quart baking dish. Beat the eggs and sugar until light. Stir in milk, nutmeg, cinnamon, and vanilla. Add raisins.

Set baking dish in a larger pan; fill with enough hot water to reach halfway up the sides of the pan. Pour milk mixture over bread cubes in baking dish.

Bake pudding in a 350°F. oven for 1¼ hours or until a knife inserted in the center of the pudding comes out clean. Cool pudding.

To serve pudding, spoon into individual dessert bowls. Serve warm or cold.

RICE PUDDING
WITH CUSTARD

SERVES 6

3 cups milk

½ cup sugar

¼ teaspoon salt

1½ cups cooked rice

4 eggs, lightly beaten

1½ teaspoons vanilla

½ cup golden raisins

In a heavy saucepan combine milk, sugar, and salt. Bring mixture to a boil over medium heat. Stir in rice. Remove from heat. Let stand for 5 minutes.

Mix eggs, vanilla, and raisins. Blend with milk mixture.

Pour pudding into a 2-quart baking dish. Bake in a 350°F. oven for 30 minutes. Stir pudding, continue baking for 30 minutes longer or until a knife inserted in the center comes out clean. Remove pudding from the oven and cool.

Serve pudding cold. Pudding is good plain, with vanilla yogurt, or with sweetened whipped cream.

SPICY BROWN RICE PUDDING

SERVES 4

4 eggs

¼ cup firmly packed light brown sugar

1 teaspoon vanilla

2 tablespoons dark rum

1 teaspoon pumpkin pie spice

¼ teaspoon ground mace

1½ cups cooked brown rice

2½ cups milk, scalded

Mix eggs, sugar, vanilla, rum, and spices. Mix in rice and add milk.

Pour mixture into a 1½-quart baking dish. Set in a larger pan and fill pan with hot water halfway up the sides of dish. Bake at 350°F. for 1 hour or until the pudding tests done, stirring once.

Serve cold. Good with berries.

DUFFS, FOOLS, FLUMMERIES

Many of these uniquely named puddings were made using fresh, pre-cooked, or stewed fruits, which was obviously a clever method in earlier days for extending the fruit season. And it is still clever to prepare these desserts in the summer when the fruits are abundant.

Duffs. These puddings are stewed fruit mixed with cookie crumbs. In the recipe included here I have combined applesauce with crushed gingersnaps.

Fools. The name apparently comes from an English use of the word as synonymous with the word *trifle*, meaning something of little importance. Thus, a fool pudding was an afterthought, a mere trifle. A fool is a purée of cooked fruit, folded into swirls of whipped cream. These desserts are very attractive when served in high, fluted glasses. A popular early English dessert was a gooseberry fool.

Flummeries. These are puddings of stewed fruit.

APPLESAUCE DUFF

SERVES 6

2 cups applesauce, homemade or canned

⅓ cup sugar

2 tablespoons grated lemon peel

2 cups plus 1 tablespoon fine gingersnap
   crumbs

1 cup heavy cream

Blend together applesauce, sugar, lemon peel, and crumbs in mixing bowl. Refrigerate until chilled.

Whip cream until firm. Using a rubber spatula, fold into applesauce mixture.

Spoon the duff into frosted glasses or dessert bowls. Serve immediately with plain cookies or shortbread.

VERY BERRY FOOL

SERVES 6

1 pint strawberries, hulled

1 pint blueberries, picked over, with any
   bruised or dried berries discarded

1 pint raspberries, picked over

1 cup sugar

1 tablespoon freshly squeezed lemon juice

1½ cups heavy cream

Simmer the fruit, sugar, and juice for 5 minutes, stirring often. Add water, by the tablespoon, if berries seem dry. Purée fruit and refrigerate until cold. Divide berries into 6 dessert bowls.

Whip cream until firm. Swirl whipped cream into each portion of berries. Serve soon.

If the fruit is very ripe just purée, chill, and marbleize with whipped cream.

BLACK AND BLUE FOOL

SERVES 6

1 quart fresh or defrosted, drained
   blackberries
1 quart fresh plums, pitted and chopped
1 cup sugar
2 tablespoons freshly squeezed orange juice
1½ cups heavy cream

Simmer blackberries and blueberries with sugar and juice for 5 minutes, stirring often. Pour berries into serving bowl and refrigerate until berries are cool.

Whip cream until firm. Spoon dollops of whipped cream onto the cool fruit. Swirl the cream into the berries. Serve soon.

GOOSEBERRY FOOL

**2 cans (16-ounces each) gooseberries, with
liquid, or fresh berries if available**

¼ cup sugar

1 cup heavy cream

⅓ cup sugar

½ teaspoon ground cinnamon

Place gooseberries in saucepan with fruit syrup and sugar. Cook over medium heat 8-10 minutes, stirring often. Mash berries while stirring. Cool. Purée.

Meanwhile, beat heavy cream sprinkled with sugar and cinnamon until soft peaks form.

Place puréed gooseberries in a dish. Spoon whipped cream over fruit purée and fold in decoratively. Bring to table and ladle into serving dishes. Good with shortbread cookies.

QUICK STRAWBERRY YOGURT FOOL

SERVES 6

1 quart strawberries, hulled

½-¾ cup sugar

2 cups low-fat vanilla yogurt

Mash the strawberries in a bowl. Mix in sugar and let berries stand for 10 minutes.

Spoon yogurt in dollops onto the mashed berries and swirl yogurt into the mixture. Chill the fool until serving time.

This recipe calls for raw egg whites; therefore, this dessert should be pre-pared within an hour of eating.

LEMON FLUMMERY

SERVES 4

1 cup water

1 tablespoon butter or margarine

Grated peel and juice of 1 lemon

2 tablespoons cornstarch

½ cup sugar

2 eggs, separated

Combine water, butter, and grated peel in a saucepan, bringing mix-ture to a boil over medium-high heat. Reduce heat to medium and continue cooking until the butter melts, stirring often.

Mix cornstarch and sugar in a bowl. Stir in butter mixture. Set aside.

Beat yolks until light. Add 2 tablespoons of the liquid. Add eggs slowly to cooked mixture in the pan. Simmer for 8 to 10 minutes, stir-ring occasionally.

Beat egg whites until stiff peaks form and reserve.

Mix lemon juice into the pudding. Pour pudding into a bowl. Cool and fold in the egg whites. Serve cold.

STRAWBERRY FLUMMERY

SERVES 6

½ cup plus 2 tablespoons sugar

3 tablespoons cornstarch

3 cups strawberries

1 cup water

2 tablespoons freshly squeezed lemon juice

Stir sugar and cornstarch together in a saucepan. Stir in berries, water, and juice. Simmer for 5 minutes, stirring often. Cool.

Spoon flummery into sauce dishes and serve cold. Serve with half-and-half if desired.

This recipe is included with permission from the Williston Memorial Library, Mount Holyoke College, South Hadley, Massachusetts, where my daughter is a student.

DEACON PORTER'S HAT

SERVES 6-8

½ cup shortening

1 cup molasses

1 cup sour milk

2 cups flour (or more)

½ teaspoon baking soda (generous)

½ teaspoon ground cinnamon

½ teaspoon ground cloves

½ teaspoon ground nutmeg

¼ cup raisins

LEMON SAUCE

½ cup sugar

1 tablespoon flour

Salt

1 cup boiling water

1 tablespoon butter

½ teaspoon lemon extract

Melt the shortening; add molasses and milk and remove from the heat. Mix and sift the flour, baking soda, and spices and add this to the shortening mixture. Stir in the raisins. The resulting batter should be stiff; add more flour if needed.

Turn the batter into buttered mold, cover, and steam for 2 hours.

To prepare the sauce, mix well the sugar, flour, and salt in a saucepan and moisten this mixture with a little cold water. Pour the boiling water over the mixture, and simmer for 5 minutes. Stir constantly until the sauce thickens. Remove the sauce from the heat and stir in the butter and lemon extract. Serve hot.

EASY TAPIOCA PUDDING

SERVES 6

2 eggs

4 tablespoons quick-cooking tapioca

½ cup sugar

2½ cups milk

1 teaspoon vanilla

Beat the eggs lightly. Mix eggs, tapioca, sugar, and milk in a saucepan. Allow pudding to stand for 5-6 minutes.

Cook pudding over medium heat until tapioca pudding comes to a boil, stirring often. Remove from heat, mix in vanilla. Cool pudding. Pour into a serving bowl.

Serve tapioca pudding cold or room temperature. For an extra treat mix 1½ cups sweetened raspberries into pudding before serving and pass milk or cream at the table.

CEREAL PUDDING

SERVES 6

2 cups milk

½ cup quick-cooking farina

⅓ cup firmly packed light brown sugar

3 eggs, slightly beaten

3 tablespoons butter or margarine

1 cup golden raisins

Blend milk, farina, sugar, and beaten eggs in a heavy saucepan. Bring pudding to a boil over medium-high heat. Reduce heat to medium and continue cooking for 4-5 minutes, stirring often. Stir in butter and raisins. Remove from heat. Cover and let stand for 5 minutes. Stir pudding and serve hot in dessert dishes.

Prepare summer pudding the night before serving. The bread absorbs the juice from the berries and becomes berry color. This recipe can easily be doubled.

BERRY SUMMER PUDDING

SERVES 4

1 package (12 ounces) frozen, unsweetened
   raspberries or blueberries
⅓ cup sugar
7-8 slices white bread with crust discarded

Defrost berries and reserve juice.

Mix berries, juice, and sugar in a bowl. Let stand 20 minutes. Cut the bread into 1-inch strips.

Use a 1-quart bowl. Ladle a cup of berries and juice in the bottom of bowl. Set bread slices firmly on top of berries. Finish layering the berries, juice, and bread in this style until all the bread and berries have been used, ending with juice. Cover tightly with aluminum foil. Set a plate that fits on top of the pudding and weight it with cans of food. Refrigerate overnight.

When ready to serve, invert onto serving dish. Spoon pudding into dessert dishes and top with yogurt or sour cream.

VANILLA PUDDING

SERVES 4

¾ cup sugar

2 tablespoons cornstarch

⅛ teaspoon salt

2½ cups milk

2 eggs plus 1 yolk, beaten

2 tablespoons butter or margarine

1½ teaspoons vanilla

Stir sugar, cornstarch, and salt in a heavy saucepan. Whisk in milk. Cook over medium heat, whisking almost constantly. Cook until pudding thickens slightly.

Remove about ¼ cup of hot pudding and slowly stir into eggs. In a slow steady stream, pour the egg mixture into pudding, stirring constantly. Continue cooking 3-4 minutes, stirring often.

Mix butter and vanilla. Cool. Pour pudding into individual dishes and refrigerate until serving time. Good with raspberry purée.

CUSTARDS

Serving a custard like mother or grandmother used to make is a great demonstration of love. It is the original comfort food. Custards are a dessert of first-rate quality, prepared by experts in the kitchen and beginners alike.

Here are some tips for making the best custard:

It is important to use the freshest eggs.

Custards are served chilled. After they are prepared, cool, cover, and refrigerate until needed.

Do not overcook custard, and do not cook it at too high a temperature. Custard tests done when a knife inserted in the center comes out clean.

The versatile custard can either be baked or cooked. Custard thickens as it sets, and so it can look looser at the end of cooking than you might expect.

A *bain marie* is a pan of water in which the cup or bowl of custard is baked. You can create a *bain marie* by using a roasting pan or any deep ovenproof dish that is large enough to hold the bowl of custard. Use hot, not boiling, water in this outer pan. The water should measure halfway up the outside of the dish of custard.

A cooked custard can be prepared in the top of a double boiler or in a heavy saucepan. Use a simmering water; do not use boiling water. And remember, stir the custard often while it is cooking. Custard is done when it is thick enough to coat the spoon.

To prevent a skin from forming, stir the custard occasionally while it is cooling. You may want to cover the custard with a grease-proof paper or plastic wrap.

Sometimes a small amount of cornstarch is added to the custard. This technique is used for making pastry cream and for thicker custards.

If using a microwave, use a *bain marie* and stir custard frequently during cooking. Cooking time varies according to individual microwaves and the amount of custard you are preparing.

CARAMEL COFFEE CUSTARD

SERVES 6

⅔ cup sugar, divided

2 cups milk

5 eggs, beaten lightly

¼ cup cooled coffee

2 teaspoons vanilla

Preheat a heavy frying pan over medium heat. Sprinkle half of sugar into hot pan. Add 2 tablespoons water and stir continuously until it is dissolved and golden in color. Working quickly, pour syrup into castle molds or custard cups. Using a pot holder, turn cups to coat bottom of molds. Set aside.

Simmer milk and remaining sugar over medium heat until sugar dissolves, stirring often. Blend eggs with coffee and vanilla. In a slow but steady stream beat in milk. Divide mixture between the prepared custard cups. Set cups in a baking dish.

Place in oven and pour hot water in pan halfway up the sides of the molds. Bake at 350°F. for 25 minutes or until they test done. Test by inserting knife in center of custard; knife should come out clean. Cool on a baking rack. Chill and serve.

COMFORT CUSTARD

⅔ cup sugar

3 tablespoons unbleached all-purpose flour

¼ teaspoon salt

6 egg yolks

4 cups milk, scalded and cooled

2 teaspoons sherry

Beat sugar with flour, salt, and egg yolks until light. In a heavy saucepan, slowly whisk egg yolk mixture into milk.

Simmer or use a double boiler over simmering water, stirring almost constantly until mixture thickens and will coat a metal spoon when inserted into the custard. Remove custard from heat. Stir in sherry. Cool until ready to use.

CHERRY CUSTARD PUDDING

SERVES 6-8

4½ cups pitted sour cherries

8 tablespoons butter, cut in ½-inch pieces

1 cup sugar

1 loaf angel cake or sponge cake, crumbled
  (3 cups crumbs)

6 eggs, separated

Place cherries with 2 tablespoons of water in a saucepan. Simmer for 4 minutes, stirring and crushing the cherries. Cool.

Cream the butter and sugar. Blend in the cherries. Mix in crumbled cake. In a separate bowl beat the egg yolks until light. Mix egg yolks into the cake batter. In another bowl beat the egg whites until stiff peaks form. Fold the egg whites into the batter.

Pour mixture into a greased 2-quart baking dish. Bake pudding in a 375°F. oven for 30-35 minutes or until pudding tests done.

Cool pudding. Serve in a deep dish dessert bowl.

MAPLE CUSTARD

SERVES 6

4 eggs

½ cup maple syrup

2 cups milk, scalded and cooled

⅛ teaspoon salt

Beat eggs until light. Mix in maple syrup. In a slow steady stream whisk egg mixture into milk. Add salt.

Pour into 6 custard cups. Place in a pan of hot water that measures halfway up the sides of the custard cups. Bake custard in a 350°F. oven for 25-30 minutes or until the custard tests done. Cool. Remove custard from the water.

Serve maple custard warm or cold, perhaps with a dusting of ground nutmeg.

Soft custard is not difficult to prepare; just treat the egg and milk mixture with the loving care it deserves. Stirred custard is a smooth and creamy mixture and is a very old recipe.

STIRRED CUSTARD

SERVES 6

4 eggs

½ cup sugar

¼ teaspoon salt

3 tablespoons all-purpose flour

2½ cups milk, scalded and cooled

1½ teaspoons vanilla

Whisk together eggs, sugar, salt, and flour until light. Pour into heavy saucepan or a double boiler over simmering water and slowly stir in milk. Continue simmering, stirring almost constantly until the mixture thickens and coats a metal spoon when inserted in the custard. Cooking time should be about 10 minutes. Remove pan from heat. Stir in vanilla.

Cool custard and pour into a bowl. Cover custard with plastic wrap to help prevent coating. Serve with fresh fruit.

MOLDED
BLACKBERRY JELLY ROLL
WITH CUSTARD

SERVES 8-10

JELLY ROLL

5 eggs

¾ cup sugar

1 teaspoon vanilla

¾ cup unbleached all-purpose flour

1 teaspoon baking powder

2 tablespoons cornstarch

1 jar (16 ounces) blackberry jelly

CUSTARD

5 egg yolks

¾ cup sugar

3 tablespoons cornstarch

2 cups milk, scalded and cooled

1½ teaspoons vanilla

2 envelopes unflavored gelatin

½ cup cold water

Beat eggs in a large bowl until light. Mix in sugar and vanilla. Sift flour, baking powder, and cornstarch. Sprinkle half of the mixture over the batter and fold in with a rubber spatula. Repeat with remaining flour mixture.

Grease and line the bottom of a 10 x 15-inch jelly roll pan with waxed paper. Spread the batter evenly in pan. Bake cake in a 400°F. oven for 12-15 minutes or until cake is a golden color and springs back when lightly touched.

Set a towel on work counter. Sprinkle lightly with sugar. Invert cake on the towel. Remove and discard paper. Carefully, roll up the cake, using the towel as a guide. The cake will be rolled jelly roll style. Cool.

When cake is cool, unroll and spread with blackberry jelly. Reroll cake. Cut cake in ½-inch slices.

Line a 2-quart domed bowl with slices. Reserve any remaining slices.

To prepare the custard, beat the egg yolks and sugar until light. Whisk in flour. Stir in milk in a slow steady stream until blended.

Pour mixture into a saucepan over medium heat. Bring to a boil, stirring constantly. Reduce heat to simmer; continue to stir for 2 minutes. Remove custard from heat. Stir in vanilla; set aside until almost cooled. Leave custard in saucepan.

Meanwhile, sprinkle gelatin over cold water and let stand for 5 minutes. Stir gelatin into the custard and simmer for 4 minutes, stirring occasionally. Cool. Ladle the custard into the bowl lined with jelly roll slices. Top with remaining cake slices if any.

Chill for 4 hours or until firm. To serve, invert onto a serving dish. Cut into wedges.

INDIVIDUAL TRIFLES

SERVES 4

CUSTARD

3 egg yolks

¼ cup sugar

2 tablespoons unbleached all-purpose flour

⅛ teaspoon salt

1¼ cups milk, scalded and cooled

¾ teaspoon vanilla

8 ladyfingers, split and cut into pieces

4 tablespoons Grand Marnier liqueur

3 egg whites

½ cup sugar

½ teaspoon vanilla

To prepare custard, beat egg yolks, ¼ cup sugar, flour, and salt until light. In a heavy saucepan slowly whisk egg yolk mixture into milk. Simmer, stirring almost constantly, until mixture thickens and will coat a metal spoon when inserted into the custard. Remove custard from heat. Stir in vanilla. Cool until ready to use.

Spoon cooled custard evenly in custard cups or ramekins. Sprinkle liqueur over ladyfingers and set over custard.

Beat the egg whites until soft peaks form. Sprinkle with sugar. Continue beating until stiff peaks form. Mix in vanilla. Cover the custard cups with the meringue. Bake trifles in a 350°F. oven until the meringue is a golden brown, about 10 minutes. Chill before serving.

TRIFLE

SERVES 8

Custard (see recipe on page 74)
8 slices day-old pound cake, about ½-inch
    thick
4 tablespoons apricot jam
¼ cup sherry
1½ cups fresh, pitted, drained apricots
1 cup whipped sweetened heavy cream
    (with ¼ cup sugar)
⅓ cup chopped candied orange peel

Prepare custard.

Spread pound cake with jam. Cut cake in 1-inch strips.

Pour half of the custard into a 2-quart serving dish. If you have a clear bowl use it. Set half of the cake strips over the custard in a single layer. Sprinkle cake with 2 tablespoons of the sherry. Sprinkle ¾ cup of the apricots over the cake. Ladle the remaining custard over the apricots. Set the remaining cake over the custard, sprinkle with sherry, top with apricots, and garnish with whipped cream. Sprinkle candied orange peel over the whipped cream.

Chill until serving time. Bring trifle to the table and spoon it into individual deep dish dessert bowls.

CHOCOLATE PUDDINGS

Hints on Chocolate Use

To store chocolate keep it cool, dry, and in an area of low humidity. Wrap chocolate airtight, as it absorbs odors. Chocolate can be stored in the refrigerator. It should be at room temperature before using it in a recipe.

A white film can form on the chocolate when it is stored in an area that has temperature changes. This "chocolate bloom" does not affect the chocolate taste. The chocolate will return to its natural color when melted.

To melt chocolate in a microwave, place chopped chocolate chips in a glass measuring cup. Microwave for 1 minute on high. Then stir chocolate, microwave for 30-40 seconds, and stir again.

To melt chocolate on a stove top, use the top of a double boiler over simmering water. Cook over medium heat, stirring as the chocolate melts.

CHOCOLATE PUDDING

SERVES 4

⅓ cup cocoa

½ cup sugar

2½ tablespoons cornstarch

2 cups milk, divided

1 teaspoon vanilla

Combine the cocoa, sugar, and cornstarch in a bowl. Mix ¼ cup of the milk into the dry ingredients.

Scald the remaining milk. Stir in cocoa mixture.

Simmer until mixture thickens, stirring often, for about 10-15 minutes. Pour into a bowl and cool. Mix in vanilla.

Spoon pudding into individual dessert dishes and chill until set. Serve pudding cold.

CHOCOLATE BREAD PUDDING

SERVES 8

4 cups bread or rolls, torn in small pieces

½ cup sliced almonds

1½ cups milk

2 squares unsweetened chocolate

4 eggs

¾ cup firmly packed light brown sugar

1 teaspoon vanilla

Toss bread pieces and almonds together. Arrange bread in a greased 1½-quart shallow baking dish.

Heat milk and chocolate together over medium heat until chocolate is melted, stirring occasionally. Set aside.

Beat eggs and sugar together. Blend in cooled chocolate mixture. Add vanilla. Ladle mixture over bread. Bake at 350°F. until pudding tests done, about 40-50 minutes.

Cool pudding before serving or serve warm. Spoon into dessert dishes. Good with chocolate ice cream.

DOUBLE CHOCOLATE PUDDING

✑

SERVES 6-8

6 tablespoons butter or margarine

1 cup sugar

3 eggs

2 cups unbleached all-purpose flour

1 cup ground almonds

1½ teaspoons baking soda

1 teaspoon baking powder

4 tablespoons cocoa

1 teaspoon vanilla

⅓ cup heavy cream

CHOCOLATE SAUCE

2 cups sugar

2 squares semisweet chocolate, broken into pieces

¾ cup half-and-half

2½ tablespoons butter or margarine

1 scant teaspoon vanilla

Cream the 6 tablespoons butter with 1 cup sugar until light. Blend in eggs. Mix in flour, almonds, baking soda, baking powder, and cocoa. Add vanilla and cream. Spoon batter into a greased 1½-quart pudding mold. Cover with greased aluminum foil or a cloth and tie securely with string.

Set on a rack in a steamer or large saucepan. Pour water halfway up the sides of bowl. Cook over high heat until water boils. Reduce heat to simmer and cover. Steam pudding 1½ hours. Check pan after 45 minutes and add more water as necessary.

While pudding is steaming, prepare sauce. Blend sugar, chocolate, half-and-half, and butter in heavy saucepan. Cook over medium heat for 10-12 minutes, or to soft-ball stage on candy thermometer, stirring almost constantly. Remove from heat. Stir in vanilla. Serve hot or warm.

Let pudding stand 5 minutes before unmolding. To unmold pudding, run a knife around the inside edge of bowl. Invert pudding onto a dish. Serve chocolate pudding warm with chocolate sauce.

SMALL
CHOCOLATE PUDDINGS
WITH RASPBERRY SAUCE

SERVES 8

3 ounces semisweet chocolate, cut in small
   pieces
1 cup milk
¾ cup bread crumbs
2 tablespoons butter or margarine
½ cup sugar
2 eggs, separated
1 teaspoon vanilla
1 cup ground almonds

RASPBERRY SAUCE

3 cups fresh or defrosted raspberries
¾ cup sugar
2 tablespoons freshly squeezed orange juice
3 tablespoons orange flavored liqueur

Melt chocolate in milk. Pour mixture over the crumbs in a bowl. Mix well and let stand 10 minutes.

Cream butter and sugar until light. Blend in egg yolks, chocolate mixture, vanilla, and almonds.

Beat egg whites until stiff. Fold into batter.

Spoon batter into eight 2½-inch-high greased molds (castle molds if available). Cover with greased aluminum foil and tie securely with string.

Set molds on a rack in a steamer or large saucepan. Pour water halfway up the sides of molds. Cook over high heat until water boils.

Reduce heat to simmer and cover. Steam pudding about 45 minutes. Check pan, adding more water as necessary.

While pudding is steaming make sauce. Purée raspberries with sugar, juice, and liqueur. Strain the sauce and discard seeds. Pour sauce into a bowl and set aside until serving time.

To unmold pudding, run a knife around the inside edges of molds. Invert on individual dishes. Pour sauce over pudding and serve.

This is a modern version of an old recipe. I find the delicate flavor of white chocolate is more pronounced if the pudding sits overnight before serving.

WHITE CHOCOLATE CLOUD PUDDING

SERVES 6-8

⅓ cup vegetable shortening

1 cup sugar

4 egg whites, slightly beaten

1½ cups unbleached all-purpose flour

1 cup cake crumbs

1 teaspon baking powder

1 teaspoon baking soda

4 ounces white baking chocolate, melted
   and cooled

1 cup golden raisins

¾ cup low-fat vanilla yogurt

CRUSHED STRAWBERRIES

3 cups hulled strawberries

½ cup sugar

1 teaspoon freshly squeezed orange juice

Cream vegetable shortening and sugar until light. Mix in egg whites. Blend in flour, cake crumbs, baking powder, and baking soda. Mix in chocolate, raisins, and yogurt.

Spoon batter into a greased 1½-quart pudding mold. Cover with greased aluminum foil and tie securely with string.

Set on a rack in steamer or large saucepan. Pour water halfway up the sides of bowl. Cook over high heat until water boils. Reduce heat to simmer and cover. Steam pudding about 1½ hours. Check pan after 45 minutes, adding more water as necessary.

While pudding is steaming, prepare sauce. Mash berries. Stir in sugar and orange juice. Refrigerate until serving time.

Let pudding stand 5 minutes before unmolding. To unmold, run a knife around the inside edge of mold. Invert pudding on dish. Cool, cover, and refrigerate 1 day before serving. Cut in thin slices. Serve with raspberry sauce.

CHOCOLATE MOUSSE

SERVES 4

6 ounces semisweet chocolate, grated

2 tablespoons water

3 egg yolks

2 tablespoons orange-flavored liqueur, such
   as Grand Marnier

1½ cups heavy cream, chilled

⅓ cup sugar

In a small saucepan melt chocolate with water, stirring until smooth, over low heat. Beat the egg yolks into the chocolate. Mix in the Grand Marnier.

Beat the heavy cream slightly. Sprinkle with sugar. Continue beating the cream until peaks form and cream thickens. Do not over beat. Fold cream gently into the chocolate mixture until evenly blended.

Spoon mousse into 4 individual dessert dishes and refrigerate for 1½ hours or until the mousse is set.

Garnish by placing a chocolate leaf on each mousse. To make garnish, grate 3 ounces dark chocolate. Melt in a heavy saucepan, stirring constantly over low heat. When the chocolate has melted, brush it on the outer side of a rose leaf. The leaf must be free of any spray or chemicals. Chill chocolate leaves until chocolate is firm. Carefully peel the leaves off the chocolate and discard, leaving a chocolate leaf. Set on a plate and refrigerate until needed.

PIES

PIES

The culinary origin of "pie" is a hazy matter. Surely many peoples and cultures used some form of pie dish in their cooking. However, nowhere is pie a more familiar and beloved dish than in England, and the English are traditionally, and probably correctly, credited with having invented pie. According to *The Oxford English Dictionary*, the word *pie* first appeared in print in England in 1303, and there is no etymologically related word known outside England.

The very earliest English pies were meat pies, made in a deep dish lined with pastry and then filled with either meat or fish and baked. However, by 1362, pie in England referred to a wide variety of possibilities, including sweet pies made commonly with fruits, raisins, nuts, and creams.

In New England, the English pie enthusiasm took hold immediately and flourished. While rocky New England is not traditionally associated with a rich agricultural history, the first Thanksgiving, celebrated in 1621, has always been identified with food and plenty, including venison, roast goose and duck, clams and eels, corn and beans, wheat bread, corn bread, leeks, wild plums, and homemade wine. The early colonists found wild fruit and many varieties of berries – strawberries, cranberries, blackberries, and blueberries – in abundance. Ever since those earliest years, New England has enjoyed a culinary tradition that is simple, hearty, and richly satisfying. New England cooking has certainly stood the test of time and has, in fact, spread its recipes and tradition westward across the country.

Sweets and desserts have always possessed great popularity in New England. The availability of maple syrup and maple sugar has probably contributed to this, as has the desire for the energy supplied by sweets during the harsh New England winters. And pie – glorious, fresh, warm, juicy pie – stands at the forefront of New England desserts.

All of the following pie recipes, particularly those earliest and most traditional New England pies, have been updated and adapted for the modern American kitchen. All ingredients are readily available in supermarkets throughout most, if not all, of the year, although some types of pies gain much through the use of seasonally available fruit.

CRUSTS AS EASY AS PIE

Tips for the Perfect Crust

It is one of my strongest convictions that the pie crust makes the pie. The creation of pie crust is an art and takes care and skill and time to perfect. I traditionally associate the most memorable pie crusts with grandmothers, who have had the time and experience to bring the preparation of the pie crust to its height and glory.

Here are some "rules of thumb" for a perfect crust.

1. Always mix dry ingredients together, and *always* sift ingredients.

2. Cut in shortening, using pastry knife or food processor fitted with steel blade, until dough resembles coarse meal.

3. If adding eggs, be sure to break them into a small bowl first to check for freshness.

4. Combine the ingredients as you cut in shortening.

5. Brrrrrr!!!! Pie crusts are most comfortable in cold company. Use cold butter or shortening; work on a cold surface if possible; chill dough before rolling out.

6. Drip, drip, drip. Add liquids by the tablespoon while stirring. If using a food processor, add liquid with the machine running. Less is more: only add liquid until dough is smooth.

7. Play ball. Turn the dough out onto a lightly floured board, pastry cloth, or marble block. If it is necessary to knead the dough to gather it together, push it away from you with the back of your hand. Then gather the dough into a ball.

8. Cover the dough with plastic wrap and refrigerate for 20-30 minutes.

9. Prepare your work surface with a light dusting of flour. Then roll out dough to desired thickness. Or moisten work surface, lay down a sheet of wax paper. Dust the paper with flour.

10. If you feel the dough sticking to the work surface, slide a large knife underneath to release the dough.

---

11. Roll the dough out so that it is larger than the pan. You can set the pan over the dough to check for correct size.

12. Some recipes call for baking the pie crust before filling it. If so, set crust in pie plate and prick bottom and sides. Cover crust with aluminum foil and add pie weights or dried beans. Bake crust according to recipe directions.

13. Always bake the pie on the center rack of the oven to insure even baking.

CREATIVE CRUST FLAVORS

Some recipes in this book call for flavored crusts. Remember, these are only suggestions. If you find a crust that works well for you, you may want to stick with it. The flip side is to let yourself be adventurous and feel free to combine different crusts with different pies.

To vary the crust according to your taste and a particular filling, add or change the crust in any of the following manners:

1. Substitute for ice water
    • Marsala wine
    • dry white wine
    • champagne
    • apple juice
    • orange juice

2. When looking for a slightly more interesting and creative crust, add a spice in small quantity, such as ½ teaspoon of pumpkin pie spice.

3. For a nut crust, add 4-6 tablespoons of ground nuts such as walnuts, hazelnuts, pecans, or almonds.

4. For orange or lemon crust, add 3 tablespoons grated peel to crust or filling ingredients.

5. Save the scraps of dough and, using a sharp knife, cut out leaf patterns to decorate outer edge of crust.

PAT-A-CRUST

1 cup unbleached all-purpose flour
½ cup butter or margarine at room
   temperature
1 egg yolk
¼ cup sugar

Process all ingredients in a food processor fitted with a steel blade. Continue processing until the ingredients are combined and a soft dough forms. This should take about 12 seconds.

Remove crust from the processor and pat the crust evenly over the bottom and up the sides of a 9-inch pie plate.

CRUMB CRUST

This is a basic recipe for using crumbs in your crusts. Some possibilities are Oreos, vanilla wafers, or gingersnaps. One hint is to press another pie pan of the same size firmly into the crumbs to distribute them evenly.

1½ cups crumbs
½ cup sugar
5 tablespoons butter or margarine, melted
   and cooled

Combine the crumbs, sugar, and butter. Press the crumb mixture firmly on the bottom and up the sides of the pie plate.

The cookie crust can be either chilled or baked. To chill the crust, set in the refrigerator for 20 minutes before filling. To bake, set pie plate with crust on center rack in oven and bake at 375°F. for 5-7 minutes. The edges will brown slightly. Remember to cool the crust before filling.

Vegetable Shortening Double Crust

This is my favorite crust because it is nice and flaky and easy to handle.

2½ cups unbleached all-purpose flour

½ teaspoon salt

⅔ cup vegetable shortening

2 tablespoons butter

7 to 10 tablespoons ice water

Mix dry ingredients together. Cut in shortening and butter, using a pastry knife or food processor fitted with a steel blade until dough resembles corn meal, combining the ingredients as you cut in the shortening. Sprinkle the water by the tablespoon, stirring until a smooth dough is formed. Gather dough into a ball. Cover with plastic wrap and refrigerate for 20-30 minutes before using.

Roll out dough on lightly floured surface or pastry cloth.

Single Crust

1¼ cups unbleached all-purpose flour

¼ teaspoon salt

6 tablespoons shortening

1 tablespoon butter

4 to 6 tablespoons cold water

Mix dry ingredients together. Cut in shortening and butter with pastry knife or food processor fitted with a steel blade until dough resembles corn meal. Combine the ingredients as you cut in the shortening. Sprinkle the water by the tablespoon, stirring until a smooth dough, not soggy, is formed. Gather dough into a ball and cover with plastic wrap. Refrigerate 20-30 minutes before using.

Roll out dough on a lightly floured surface or pastry cloth.

CANOLA OIL CRUST

2¼ cups unbleached all-purpose flour

½ teaspoon ground cinnamon

2 tablespoons grated orange peel

½ cup canola oil

7 to 10 tablespoons ice water

Mix dry ingredients together. Blend in oil, combining ingredients as you blend. Sprinkle the water by the tablespoon, stirring until a smooth dough, not soggy, is formed. Gather dough together in a ball. Cover with plastic wrap and refrigerate 20-30 minutes before using.

Roll out the dough on a lightly floured surface or pastry cloth.

SHORT DOUGH BUTTER CRUST

2¼ cups unbleached all-purpose flour

8 tablespoons butter

¼ teaspoon salt

1 tablespoon sugar

3 tablespoons vegetable shortening

5 to 7 tablespoons ice water

Mix dry ingredients together. Cut in shortening using a pastry knife or food processor fitted with a steel blade. Sprinkle water over the dough by tablespoons, stirring until a smooth dough is formed. Gather dough into a ball. Cover with plastic wrap and refrigerate 20-30 minutes before using.

Roll out the dough on a lightly floured surface or pastry cloth.

Country Crust

2¼ cups unbleached all-purpose flour

½ teaspoon salt

⅔ cup lard

1 teaspoon cider vinegar

7 to 10 tablespoons ice water

Mix dry ingredients together. Cut in shortening using a pastry knife or food processor fitted with a steel blade until dough resembles corn meal. Combine ingredients as you cut in the lard. Sprinkle the vinegar and water slowly over the dough, stirring until a smooth dough is formed. Gather dough into a ball and cover with plastic wrap. Refrigerate 20-30 minutes before using.

Roll out the dough on a lightly floured surface or pastry cloth.

Scone Crust

3 cups cake flour, sifted

⅓ cup sugar

1 tablespoon baking powder

¼ teaspoon salt

2 tablespoons grated orange peel

9 tablespoons butter, cut in small pieces

1½ cups half-and-half

Working quickly, mix the sifted flour with sugar, baking powder, salt, and orange peel. Cut in butter with pastry knife.

Stir in half-and-half. Place dough in a bowl and refrigerate for 20 minutes. Dough will be soft and crumbly. Place dough on pastry cloth and cover with wax paper for easy handling. Pat dough, using finger tips, into two 9-inch pie plates.

Add filling and bake as directed in individual recipe or use your own fruit filling.

MERINGUE TOPS AND CRUSTS

Cover a cookie sheet with aluminum foil when shaping a meringue pie crust. Draw a 9- or 10-inch circle on the paper using a pie plate as a guide. Mound the beaten meringue on the circle. The center of the crust should be about 1-inch thick to support the filling. With the back of a spoon, shape the rim of the crust about 2 inches high.

Bake crust 1 hour in a 250°F. oven. Without opening the door, turn off the heat and leave the crust in the oven until it cools completely, about 1½ hours. Carefully remove and discard the paper. Set the crust on serving plate and fill the center.

To make a meringue top for a pie, mound the meringue evenly over the cooled filling. Seal the meringue to the crust and have the meringue higher in the center of the pie. Bake the topping in a 350°F. oven for 12-15 minutes or until the meringue is baked to a golden brown on the peaks.

Hints for a Perfect Meringue

1. Egg whites should be at room temperature.

2. Beat egg whites with salt and cream of tartar until foaming.

3. Add sugar slowly, sprinkling it over the soft peaks of meringue. Do not add too much sugar. Continue beating until firm peaks form.

4. All kitchen tools should be grease free.

5. Do not have even a trace of yolk in the egg whites.

SUMMER/AUTUMN PIES

The best known and most popular of all New England pies are made with fruits and berries. Apple pie must certainly be the dessert favorite of New England and maybe even of the country. Most fruits and berries are abundant from early summer through fall, and, while canned and dried fruits are satisfactory ingredients, nothing has the appeal and taste of fresh fruit or berry pies.

Apples are generally divided into eating and cooking types, although many eating apples are excellent for cooking.

Apples are available year round, but they are at their peak from September through November. In selecting apples, three conditions should be considered: the feel, the color, and the fragrance. Look for apples that are firm and clean; the best cooking apples are hard. The skin should be smooth and brightly colored, whether yellow, green, or red. Finally, apples should have a fresh fragrance; avoid apples that have a musty smell. Apples will keep well for about two weeks if stored either in a cool, dry place or in the refrigerator.

Cooking and baking apples should remain flavorful and firm after cooking. I particularly recommend Northern Spy, Rome Beauty, and Winesap apples, which are red, and Rhode Island Greening and Granny Smith apples, which are green, for baking pies. McIntosh, although my favorite eating apple, is not suitable for baking, as it has too much moisture. Sometimes I add one or two of them to a pie.

New Englanders know that apple pie is perfect when served with a slice of Vermont cheddar cheese. If you must have an alternative, serve the pie with a scoop of the very best vanilla ice cream.

DEEP DISH APPLE PIE

SERVES 6

10-inch double pie crust, unbaked

5 cups peeled and sliced Granny Smith apples

4 cups peeled and sliced Jonathan apples

¾ cup sugar

¼ cup unbleached all-purpose flour

1½ teaspoons ground cinnamon

¼ teaspoon ground nutmeg

1 teaspoon grated lemon peel

3 tablespoons butter or margarine, cut in
   small pieces

1 slightly beaten egg white

Sugar

Roll out half of the dough into a 12-inch circle. Place dough in a 10-inch pie plate, patting the dough with your fingers until it extends just past the edges of the pie plate. Firm down the edges of the crust. Set aside.

Toss apple slices with sugar, flour, cinnamon, nutmeg, peel, and butter. Spread apples into the pie crust, mounding the apples higher in the center.

Roll out top crust large enough to fit comfortably over the pie. Moisten the edges of the bottom crust with water. Lift top crust carefully and center it on the apple filling. Fold top crust edges under the bottom edges, sealing securely. Flute the edges of the crust. A fork pressing the crusts together works well. Brush crust with egg white and sprinkle with sugar. Make a ½-inch air vent in the center of the pie. Cover the outer edges of the crust with aluminum foil to prevent scorching.

Bake in a 375°F. oven for 35 minutes. Remove foil and continue baking for 25 minutes or until pie is done. The fruit will be tender and the crust a golden brown. Cool pie on rack. Serve apple pie room temperature or warm with thin slices of Vermont cheddar cheese.

Apple Cheese Pie

SERVES 6

9-inch single pie crust, unbaked

5 cups peeled and thinly sliced Granny
  Smith apples

½ cup sugar

½ teaspoon ground cinnamon

1 package (8 ounces) cream cheese at room
  temperature

¼ cup granulated sugar

1 egg

¾ teaspoon vanilla

Confectioner's sugar

Roll out pastry dough to about an 11-inch circle. Set the dough in pie plate, patting the dough with finger tips until it covers the edges of the pan. Firm down the edges of the crust. Crimp edges. Set aside.

Toss the apples with sugar and cinnamon. Reserve.

Blend together the cream cheese, granulated sugar, and egg. Mix in vanilla. Spread the cheese filling into the crust. Arrange the apples over the filling, mounding the apples in the center of the pie.

Bake the pie in the center of a 450°F. oven for 10 minutes. Reduce the temperature to 400°F. and continue baking for 25 minutes or until the apples are tender and the crust a golden brown. Cool pie on a rack. Sprinkle pie with confectioner's sugar before serving.

Paper bag pie comes out gorgeous and perfect every time and leaves you with a clean oven, no spills. Important: do not use a bag made of recycled paper, as it has colored ink. Use only a bag with no ink markings.

PAPER BAG
GREEN APPLE PIE

SERVES 6-8

9-inch single pie crust, unbaked

7 cups chopped cooking apples such as
   Granny Smith

½ cup sugar

¼ cup unbleached all-purpose flour

1 teaspoon ground cinnamon

¼ teaspoon ground nutmeg

1½ tablespoons freshly squeezed lemon juice

TOPPING

8 tablespoons butter or margarine, cut into
   ½-inch pieces

½ cup unbleached all-purpose flour

½ cup firmly packed light brown sugar

1 heavy brown paper grocery bag, large
   enough to hold pie loosely

12 ounces cheddar cheese

Roll out the pastry dough to an 11-inch circle. Place dough in a pie plate, patting the dough with your fingers until it extends just past the edge of the rim of the pan. Set aside.

Toss apples, sugar, flour, cinnamon, nutmeg, and lemon juice in large mixing bowl. Mound into the pie plate.

Put butter, flour, and brown sugar in food processor and pulse until topping is coarsely ground or mix topping in a bowl. Sprinkle streusel over the pie, patting it down around the edges.

Slip the pie into the paper bag, folding ends securely and closing tightly with paper clips. Place on cookie sheet on center rack. Bake pie at 375°F. for 55 minutes. Remove pie from oven. Slit bag open and take out pie. Cool on rack. Serve warm with a slice of cheddar cheese.

APPLE MINCE PIE

SERVES 6-8

9-inch double pie crust, unbaked

4 large Granny Smith apples, peeled, cored
  and chopped

2 tablespoons unbleached all-purpose flour

½ cup sugar

½ teaspoon ground cinnamon

¼ teaspoon ground allspice

¼ teaspoon ground mace

1½ tablespoons grated lemon peel

3 tablespoons orange marmalade

2 tablespoons freshly squeezed lemon juice

2 tablespoons rum or brandy

1½ cups raisins

¾ cup dried currants

½ cup chopped candied orange peel

2 egg yolks, lightly beaten

1 slightly beaten egg white

Sugar

Roll out half of the dough to about an 11-inch circle. Place dough in a pie plate, patting the dough with your fingers until it extends just past the edges of the pie plate. Crimp edges. Set aside.

Mix the chopped apples with the flour in a large, deep bowl. Toss apples with sugar, cinnamon, allspice, and mace. Mix in peel, marmalade, juice, and rum. Blend in raisins, currants, orange peel, and egg yolks. Spoon filling into the crust.

Roll out top crust large enough to fit comfortably over the pie. Moisten the edges of the bottom crust with water. Set the top crust in place over the pie. Press the edges of the pie sealing them together. Tuck pastry under edges. Press the edges of the pie lightly to seal. Make a ½-inch air vent in the center of the pie and/or 1 to 2 slits. Brush pie with egg white and sprinkle lightly with sugar. Cover edges of pie with aluminum foil, to be removed after 20 minutes of baking.

Preheat oven to 450°F. Place the pie on the center rack in the oven and lower heat to 350°F. Bake pie for 45 minutes or until the crust is golden brown. Serve pie warm, cold, or at room temperature.

THE BEST
BANANA CREAM PIE

SERVES 6-8

9-inch pie crust, baked

2 cups milk

¾ cup sugar

⅛ teaspoon salt

3 eggs, separated

3 tablespoons cornstarch

2 tablespoons butter or margarine

1 teaspoon vanilla or light rum

2 large ripe bananas, sliced just before serving

¼ teaspoon cream of tartar

¼ cup sugar

½ teaspoon vanilla

Roll out the pastry dough to an 11-inch circle. Place dough in pie plate, patting the dough with your fingers until it extends just past the edge of the rim of the pan. Firm down the edges of the crust. Prick the crust in several places and set a sheet of aluminum foil over the crust, pressing it down against the dough to help dough keep its shape during baking. Cover foil with pie weights or dry beans. Bake crust in the center of a 425°F. oven for 10 minutes. Remove foil and weights and bake 5 more minutes. Remove crust from the oven. Cool.

Scald milk with ¾ cup sugar and salt. Cool. Beat egg yolks with cornstarch. Spoon 3 tablespoons of the milk into the egg mixture. In a slow steady stream whisk the eggs into milk. Cook over medium heat until custard thickens slightly, stirring often. Remove from heat. Stir in butter and vanilla. Slice the bananas into custard. Cool. Pour filling into crust.

To make meringue beat egg whites with cream of tartar until soft peaks form. Sprinkle ¼ cup sugar over meringue and beat until sugar has been incorporated and stiff peaks form. Mix in vanilla.

Mound meringue over pie, sealing edges. Bake in a 350°F. oven for 12-14 minutes. Meringue will be golden brown on top. Cool on wire rack. Serve cold. If you like, you can serve with vanilla yogurt or sweetened whipped cream instead of the meringue.

BLACKBERRY LATTICE PIE

SERVES 6

9-inch single orange crust, baked

4 cups blackberries, washed, picked over, and
    drained on paper towels

⅓ cup granulated sugar

3 tablespoons cornstarch

3 tablespoons water

⅓ cup blackberry jam

MERINGUE LATTICE

3 egg whites at room temperature

½ cup confectioner's sugar

1 teaspoon vanilla

Roll out the pastry dough to an 11-inch circle. Place dough in a pie plate, patting the dough with your fingers until it extends just past the edge of the rim of the pan. Firm down the edge of the crust. Prick the crust in several places and set a sheet of aluminum foil over the crust, pressing it down against the dough to help the dough keep its shape during baking. Cover foil with pie weights or dry beans. Bake the crust in the center of a 425° F. oven for 10 minutes or until baked. Remove foil and weights and bake 5 more minutes. Remove crust from the oven. Cool.

Toss blackberries with granulated sugar and drain in a colander over a saucepan. Heat the juice. Stir cornstarch with 3 tablespoons water and mix into the juice. Bring mixture to a boil, stirring often. Reduce sauce to simmer and continue cooking. Stir often until thickened. Mix in berries. Heat jam with 1 tablespoon water in a saucepan. Brush jam over bottom of the crust. Mound berries in the crust.

Prepare meringue by beating egg whites until soft peaks form. Sprinkle half of the confectioner's sugar over meringue. Continue beating, incorporating the sugar. Sprinkle remaining sugar over the egg whites and continue beating until all the sugar has been absorbed. Mix in vanilla. Meringue should have stiff peaks. Spoon meringue into a pastry bag with a ½-inch opening. Make a lattice design over top of the pie.

Bake pie in the center of a 325°F. oven for 12-15 minutes or until the peaks of the meringue are a golden brown. Cool pie on rack. Serve blackberry pie cold.

For added flavor you may slice a large cooking apple and mix it in with the blueberry filing.

OLD-FASHIONED BLUEBERRY PIE

SERVES 6

9-inch double pie crust, unbaked

4 cups fresh blueberries

¼ cup unbleached all-purpose flour

½ cup granulated sugar

¼ teaspoon salt

1 tablespoon freshly squeezed lemon juice

¼ cup firmly packed light brown sugar

2 tablespoons butter or margarine

1 slightly beaten egg white

Sugar

Roll out half of the dough into an 11-inch circle. Place dough in a pie plate, patting the dough with your fingers until it extends just past the edges of the pie plate. Firm down the edges of the crust. Set aside.

Wash and pick over fresh berries. Toss with flour, granulated sugar, salt, and juice. Let stand for 5 minutes. Mound berries into the pie crust. Sprinkle brown sugar over the blueberries. Cut butter in small pieces and sprinkle over berries.

Roll out remaining top crust large enough to fit comfortably over the pie. Moisten the edges of the bottom crust with water. Set the top crust in place over the pie. Press the edges of the pie sealing together. Tuck pastry under edges. Press the edges of the pie to seal. Make a ½-inch air vent and 2 slits in center of the pie. Brush pie with egg white and sprinkle with sugar. Place strips of aluminum foil around the edges to prevent scorching.

Bake pie in a 425°F. oven on the center rack. Remove foil after 20 minutes and continue baking until crust is a golden brown and the berries' juice is bubbling, about 15-20 minutes later. Cool pie on rack. Blueberry pie is good alone or with sweetened whipped cream.

BLUEBERRY PIE IN A PAT-A-CRUST

SERVES 6

Pat-A-Crust (see page 93)

5 cups fresh blueberries, washed, picked over,
   and drained on paper toweling

2 teaspoons grated lemon peel

¼ cup sugar

Bake the pie crust in a 350°F. oven for 35 minutes. Remove from the oven and cool.

Toss the blueberries with the lemon peel and sugar. Mound the blueberries into the crust and bake for an additional 10 minutes. Serve hot or cold.

TART CHERRY PIE

SERVES 6

9-inch double pie crust, unbaked

5 cups pitted tart (sour) cherries

3 tablespoons instant tapioca

1 cup sugar

4 teaspoons ground mace

¼ teaspoon ground cardamom

2 tablespoons butter, cut into small pieces

2 tablespoons milk

Sugar

Roll out half of the dough to an 11-inch circle. Place dough in a pie plate, patting the dough with your fingers until it extends just past the edges of the pie plate. Firm down edges. Set aside.

Toss together cherries, tapioca, 1 cup sugar, mace, and cardamom. Spread the filling into the pie crust, mounding the cherries in the center of the crust. Dot pie with butter.

Roll out the remaining top crust large enough to fit comfortably over the pie. Moisten the edges of the bottom crust with water. Place top crust over the pie. Crimp and seal edges. Cut a ½-inch air vent and 2 slashes on top of the pie. Brush top of pie crust with milk and sprinkle with remaining sugar.

Bake the pie in a 375°F. oven for 55-60 minutes or until fruit is cooked and the crust is a golden brown. Cool pie on rack. Cherry pie is good warm or cold, but best served with vanilla ice cream.

Cranberries are available late in the year, from September through December. Fresh cranberries should be firm and plump. Cranberries can be refrigerated in a plastic bag for two months or frozen up to a year.

CRANBERRY MINCEMEAT PIE

SERVES 6

9-inch double pie crust, unbaked
2½ cups mincemeat (see recipe on page 162
 or use prepared mincemeat)
2¼ cups cranberry relish
2 tablespoons brandy
1¼ cups chopped walnuts or pecans
2 tablespoons butter or margarine, melted
1 egg white
Sugar

Roll out half of the dough into an 11-inch circle. Place dough in a pie plate, patting the dough with your fingers until it extends just past the edges of the pie plate. Firm down the edges of the crust. Set aside.

Mix mincemeat, cranberry relish, and brandy together. Toss walnuts with butter and mix into filling. Spoon cranberry filling into the crust.

Roll out the top crust large enough to fit comfortably over the pie. Moisten the edges of the bottom crust with water. Lift top crust carefully and center it on the filling. Fold top crust edges under the bottom edges sealing securely. Flute the edges of the crust. A fork pressing the crusts together works well. Brush crust with egg white and sprinkle with sugar.

Make a ½-inch air vent in the center of the pie. Cover the outer edges of the crust with aluminum foil to prevent scorching.

Bake the pie in a 375°F. oven for 20 minutes. Remove foil and continue baking for 35 minutes or until pie is done. The crust will be a golden brown. Cool pie on rack. Serve pie cold.

COCONUT PIE

SERVES 6

9-inch single pie crust, unbaked

6 tablespoons butter or margarine at room
   temperature

1 cup sugar

3 eggs

¾ teaspoon vanilla

½ cup golden raisins

¾ cup chopped hazelnuts

½ cup shredded coconut

Roll out pastry dough to an 11-inch circle. Place dough in pie plate patting with your fingers until it extends just past the edge of the rim of the pan. Firm down edges of the crust. Set aside.

Cream butter and sugar until light. Add eggs one at a time, beating well after each addition. Add vanilla. Mix in raisins, hazelnuts, and coconut. Pour filling into pie shell.

Bake pie in a 350°F. oven for 40-45 minutes or until pie tests done. Cool pie on rack. Serve in thin slices.

LEMON MERINGUE PIE

SERVES 6

9-inch crust, baked

1 cup sugar

3 tablespoons cornstarch

2 tablespoons flour

¼ teaspoon salt

1½ cups water

1½ tablespoons butter

3 egg yolks, slightly beaten

5 tablespoons freshly squeezed lemon juice

2 tablespoons lemon zest

MERINGUE

4 egg whites at room temperature

½ cup sugar

¼ teaspoon cream of tartar

Roll out the pastry dough to an 11-inch circle. Place the dough in a pie plate, patting the dough with your fingers until it extends just past the edge of the rim of the pan. Firm down the edges of the crust. Prick the crust in several places and set a sheet of aluminum foil over the crust, pressing it down against the dough to help the dough keep its shape during baking. Cover foil with pie weights or dry beans. Bake crust in the center of a 425°F. oven for 10 minutes. Remove foil and weights and bake 5 minutes longer. Remove crust from the oven. Cool.

In a saucepan combine sugar, cornstarch, flour, salt, and water. Cook over medium heat until mixture begins to boil. Stirring, continue cooking, simmering for about 3 minutes, or until mixture thickens.

Remove from heat. Mix in butter. Carefully stir 4 tablespoons of the sauce, 1 tablespoon at a time, into the egg yolks, beating well after each addition. In a slow steady stream, mix egg yolks into the sauce, whisking constantly. Stir in lemon juice and zest. Return pan to medium-low heat. Continue cooking 2 minutes, whisking constantly. Cool filling. Spoon it into the prepared crust. Filling will be thick.

To prepare meringue, beat egg whites until soft peaks form. Sprinkle egg whites with sugar and cream of tartar. Continue beating, incorporating sugar until stiff peaks form. Mound meringue on top of warm pie filling, sealing the edges and mounding meringue in the center of the pie.

Bake the pie in a 350°F. oven for 8-10 minutes or until the meringue has golden peaks. Cool pie on rack. Serve pie cold.

ORANGE MERINGUE PIE

SERVES 6

9-inch single pie crust, baked

½ cup plus 2 tablespoons sugar

6 tablespoons cornstarch

¼ teaspoon salt

1¾ cups milk

4 eggs, separated

1 cup freshly squeezed orange juice

3 tablespoons freshly squeezed lemon juice

¼ cup sugar

¼ teaspoon cream of tartar

Roll out pastry dough to an 11-inch circle. Place the dough in a pie plate, patting the dough with your fingers until it extends just past the edge of the rim of the pan. Firm down the edges of the crust. Prick the crust in several places and set a sheet of aluminum foil over the crust, pressing it down against the dough to help the dough keep its shape during baking. Cover foil with pie weights or dry beans. Bake crust in the center of a 425° F. oven for 10 minutes. Remove foil and weights and bake 5 more minutes or until crust is a light golden brown. Cool.

Mix together the ½ cup plus 2 tablespoons sugar, cornstarch, and salt in a medium saucepan. Mix in the milk and simmer, stirring often until the sauce thickens. Beat egg yolks in a small bowl until light. Add 3 tablespoons milk slowly into the egg yolks. In a slow steady stream, pour egg yolk into the milk mixture whisking until incorporated. Whisk in orange and lemon juice. Continue cooking over simmering heat, whisking until sauce thickens. Cool. Pour filling into the baked pie crust. Chill until the filling is firm.

To prepare meringue, beat the egg whites with the cream of tartar until soft peaks form. Sprinkle sugar over egg whites; continue beating until stiff peaks form. Mound the meringue over chilled pie, sealing the edges with meringue.

Bake the pie in a 350°F. oven for 10 minutes or until the meringue is a golden brown. Cool pie on rack. Serve at room temperature.

Peaches are generally available throughout the country from May to October, although their peak season is in July and August. In selecting peaches, look for intensely fragrant fruit, possessing a fresh, bright color. Peaches bruise easily, and, while ripe peaches should give slightly with palm pressure, avoid overly soft peaches or those with bruised skins.

Peaches do not keep long at room temperature, so I recommend buying only enough to use in a particular recipe. However, peaches will keep for several days if refrigerated in a plastic bag.

PEACH STREUSEL PIE

SERVES 6

9-inch single pastry crust, unbaked

5 cups peeled and sliced peaches

1 cup chopped dates

3 tablespoons instant tapioca

½ cup granulated sugar

¼ teaspoon ground nutmeg

¾ cup firmly packed light brown sugar

⅓ cup unbleached all-purpose flour

¼ cup butter or margarine, cut in small pieces

½ cup ground pecans

Roll out the pastry dough to about an 11-inch circle. Place dough in a pie plate, patting the dough with your fingers until it extends just past the edge of the rim of the pan. Firm down the edges of the crust. Crimp edges. Set aside.

Toss peaches and dates with the tapioca, granulated sugar, and nutmeg. Mound the peach filling into the pie crust.

Mix together the brown sugar, flour, butter, and pecans. Sprinkle the streusel mixture over the pie.

Bake peach pie in a 375°F. oven for 50 minutes or until the fruit is tender and the crust is a golden brown. Cool pie on rack. Serve pie warm, plain or with peach ice cream.

PLUM GINGER PIE

SERVES 6

9-inch double lemon crust, unbaked

6 cups fresh purple plums, washed, pitted,
  and chopped

1 tablespoon candied ginger

¼ cup instant tapioca

½ teaspoon ground cinnamon

¼ teaspoon ground ginger

2 tablespoons grated lemon peel

2 tablespoons butter or margarine, cut in
  small pieces

Roll out the pastry dough into an 11-inch circle. Place dough in a pie plate, patting the dough with your fingers until it extends just past the edge of the rim of the pie plate. Firm down the edges of the crust. Set aside.

Toss chopped plums, candied ginger, tapioca, cinnamon, ground ginger, and peel together. Mound filling into pie crust.

Roll out top crust large enough to fit over the pie. Moisten edges of bottom crust with water. Lift top crust carefully and center it on the filling. Seal with bottom layer. Fold top crust under bottom crust sealing securely and flute the edges of the crust. A fork pressing the crusts together works well. Make a ½-inch vent in the center of the pie. Cover edges of crust with aluminum foil to prevent scorching.

Bake the pie in the center of the oven at 375°F. for 50 minutes or until plums are tender and the crust is a golden brown. Remove foil after 20 minutes of baking. Cool pie on rack. Serve with vanilla ice cream.

This pie is a treasured recipe from my Aunt Ida's collection.

RASPBERRY CHEESE PIE

SERVES 6-8

9-inch Oreo or other crumb crust, unbaked

1 package (8 ounces) cream cheese at room
   temperature, cut in thirds

8 ounces cream-style cottage cheese

¾ cup sugar

2 eggs

3 tablespoons cornstarch

2 teaspoons freshly squeezed lemon juice

1 teaspoon vanilla

¼ cup butter or margarine, melted and cooled

½ cup sour cream

3 cups fresh raspberries, picked over, washed,
   and drained on paper toweling

¼ cup currant jelly

2 tablespoons water

Prepare crust and set aside.

Beat cream cheese with cottage cheese, sugar, and eggs until light, about 10 minutes with an electric mixer. Add lemon juice and vanilla. Mix in butter and sour cream. Continue beating until thoroughly blended.

Pour filling into prepared crust. Bake pie in a 325°F. oven, on the center rack, for 1 hour or until the pie tests done and is firm to the touch. Turn off oven. Leave the pie in the oven for 1½ hours with the door closed. Remove the pie from the oven. Cool completely. Refrigerate at least 6 hours before serving.

Make the topping before serving. Arrange the raspberries (or other fruit of your choice) decoratively on the top of the pie. Heat jelly with water, stirring to make a liquid. Cool. Brush jelly over the tops of the berries. Serve pie cold.

Although both rhubarb and strawberries are fruits of the spring, this pie can be prepared in the winter using frozen rhubarb and strawberries.

RHUBARB STRAWBERRY PIE

SERVES 6

9-inch double pie crust, unbaked

4 cups sliced (½-inch) rhubarb with leaves
   discarded

1 cup sugar

3 tablespoons quick-cooking tapioca

½ teaspoon ground cinnamon

2 tablespoons freshly squeezed orange juice

1 cup crushed fresh strawberries or
   defrosted berries

3 tablespoons butter or margarine, cut in
   ½-inch pieces

1 slightly beaten egg white

Sugar

Roll out half of the dough into an 11-inch circle. Place dough into a 9-inch pie plate, patting the dough with your fingers until it extends just past the edges of the pie plate. Firm down the edges of the crust. Set aside.

Place the cut rhubarb in a large bowl. Mix the 1 cup sugar, tapioca, and cinnamon in a separate small bowl. Toss the sugar mixture with the rhubarb. Stir the orange juice with the strawberries. Mix the strawberries with the rhubarb and the butter pieces. Spread the fruit in the pie crust, mounding the fruit somewhat higher in the center of the crust.

Roll out the top crust large enough to fit comfortably over the pie. Moisten the edges of the bottom crust with water. Lift the top crust carefully and center it on the rhubarb filling. Fold top crust edges under the bottom edges, sealing securely. Flute the edges of the crust. A fork pressing the crusts together works well. Brush crust with egg white and sprinkle with sugar. Make a ½-inch air vent in the center of the pie. Cover the outer edges of the crust with aluminum foil to prevent scorching.

Bake the pie in a 425°F. oven for 20 minutes. Remove foil and continue baking for 30-35 minutes or until pie is done. The fruit will be tender and the crust a golden brown. Cool pie on rack. Serve Rhubarb Strawberry Pie at room temperature.

STRAWBERRY PIE

SERVES 6

9-inch single pie crust, baked

1½ tablespoons cornstarch

½ cup plus 2 tablespoons of cold water

2 cups boiling water

1¾ cup sugar

⅛ teaspoon salt

5 cups hulled strawberries, washed

SWEETENED WHIPPED CREAM

1 cup heavy cream

3 tablespoons sugar

1 teaspoon vanilla

Roll out the pastry dough to an 11-inch circle. Place the dough in a pie plate, patting the dough with your fingers until it extends just past the edge of the rim of the pan. Firm down the edges of the crust. Prick the crust in several places and set a sheet of aluminum foil over the crust, pressing it down against the dough to help the dough keep its shape during baking. Cover foil with pie weights or dry beans. Bake crust in the center of a 425°F. oven for 10 minutes. Remove foil and weights and bake 5 more minutes. Remove crust from the oven. Cool.

Dissolve the cornstarch in the ½ cup plus 2 tablespoons cold water. Bring 2 additional cups of water to a boil. Stir in the dissolved cornstarch and continue boiling for 2 minutes. Stir in the 1¾ cups sugar and continue boiling to soft ball stage on candy thermometer. Stir in salt.

Cool to room temperature. Add strawberries and mix well. Pour filling into baked pie crust. Chill 1 hour before serving. Filling will be soft.

Whip the cream until it begins to thicken. Sprinkle with sugar and continue beating until the cream is firm. Mix in vanilla.

Serve Strawberry Pie with Sweetened Whipped Cream.

When it came time to test this pie the only green tomatoes that were available were the green cherry tomatoes harvested from daughter Dorothy's tomato plant. So with due respect to the whole tomato, these cherry tomatoes worked perfectly fine. Thank you, Dorothy.

GREEN TOMATO PIE

SERVES 6

9-inch lattice pastry crust, unbaked

3-4 cups sliced green tomatoes (if using
   cherry tomatoes, cut them in half)

2 tablespoons freshly squeezed lemon juice

1 tablespoon grated lemon peel

¼ teaspoon salt

¾ teaspoon ground cinnamon

¼ teaspoon ground mace

⅔ cup sugar

3 tablespoons cornstarch

2 tablespoons butter or margarine

Roll out half of the pastry dough to an 11-inch circle. Place dough in a pie plate, patting the dough with your fingers until it extends just past the edge of the rim of the pan. Firm down the edge of the crust. Set aside.

To make the filling, toss tomatoes with juice, peel, salt, cinnamon, and mace in a saucepan. Cook tomatoes over low heat, uncovered, for 3 minutes, stirring often. Tomatoes should be cooked but still firm.

Mix sugar and cornstarch together. Mix sugar into tomato filling. Continue cooking until mixture thickens slightly. Stir in butter and mix until butter has melted. Pour filling into pie plate.

With remaining crust, roll out and cut into ½-inch strips using a sharp knife. Set half of the strips 1 inch apart over the filling. Weave remaining strips over filling in opposite direction. Press lattice strips firmly into the edge of pie.

Bake in a 425°F. oven for 40 minutes or until the crust is a golden brown. Cool on rack. Serve at room temperature.

YOGURT PIES

Yogurt is booming in popularity, mainly due to its health benefits. It is rich in B vitamins, protein, and calcium, and its lowered fat content makes it preferable to richer dairy products. We have used yogurt as a basis for frozen pies and gelatin-based pies, and we made a simple yogurt cheese and used it for a yogurt cheese pie.

It is interesting to note how quickly a single ingredient can become an integral addition to the cooking of a locale or a people. Molasses, for instance, was obviously not native to New England, but the import of molasses into New England from the West Indies in the late seventeenth century caused an explosion of culinary applications. Molasses became a key ingredient in a variety of New England recipes. In the last 25 years, yogurt likewise has burgeoned in popularity in New England, as well as in the rest of the country, and is now a staple in many dishes and an increasingly favorite ingredient in puddings and pies.

YOGURT BANANA PIE

SERVES 6

9-inch vanilla cookie crust, chilled

2 ripe bananas

¼ cup firmly packed light brown sugar

1½ cups creamed cottage cheese

2 cups yogurt, vanilla or banana

1 teaspoon vanilla

¼ teaspoon ground nutmeg

Prepare cookie crust and set aside.

Slice bananas then toss them with the sugar. Spread bananas evenly over bottom of the pie crust.

In large bowl of electric mixer, beat cottage cheese, yogurt, vanilla, and nutmeg until smooth, about 6 minutes. Force the filling through a sieve. Spoon yogurt filling into the pie crust.

Cover pie lightly with foil. Freeze pie for 2 hours before serving. Have pie at room temperature to soften slightly before serving.

Most berries peak in early summer, from June to July. Strawberries, blueberries, raspberries, and other soft berries should be used on the day of purchase. Look for bright-colored berries which are firm and dry. Always avoid purchasing berries which are packaged in wet or stained containers, if possible. Do not wash berries until you are ready to use them. Store berries in the refrigerator in moistureproof containers or on a tray lined with a paper towel. When ready to use them put berries in a colander or sieve and run cold water over them gently; drain the berries thoroughly.

YOGURT GELATIN BLUEBERRY PIE

SERVES 6

9-inch cookie (oatmeal or granola) crust, chilled

2 packages (3 ounces each) raspberry jello

2 cups boiling water

½ cup cold water

2 cups blueberry yogurt, mixed

1 cup fresh or defrosted, drained blueberries

Prepare crust and chill for 20 minutes. Set aside.

Pour gelatin in a mixing bowl. Stir in boiling water and mix until smooth. Blend in cold water and set aside, cooling the gelatin mixture to room temperature. Stir in the blended yogurt.

Place the filling in the refrigerator and chill until almost set, about 1 hour. Mix in the fresh blueberries. Mound the filling into the pie crust.

Refrigerate 2 to 3 hours or until pie is firm.

When grating chocolate make sure that the block of chocolate is not too cold. Use a potato peeler, scrape curls directly from the piece of chocolate.

BROWNIE YOGURT PIE

SERVES 8

**Brownie recipe (see recipe on page 177),
with 1 cup chopped walnuts added to
batter before baking**
9-inch chocolate cookie crust, chilled
3 cups vanilla yogurt
1 package sugar-free hot cocoa mix

Make brownies and cool.

Prepare cookie crust and set aside.

Mix yogurt with cocoa mix. Crumble 2 cups of the brownies and blend into the yogurt.

Mound filling into chocolate cookie crust. Cover lightly with foil. Freeze pie for 2 hours or until firm.

Remove pie and let stand at room temperature to soften slightly before serving. Serve pie with slices of remaining brownies. Garnish pie with chocolate curls if desired.

Yogurt Lemon Pie

SERVES 6-8

9-inch vanilla cookie crust, chilled

3 cups lemon yogurt

1 tablespoon grated lemon peel

1 cup non-dairy topping or sweetened
whipped cream

Prepare crust. Refrigerate for 20 minutes or longer.

Mix together the lemon yogurt, lemon peel, and 1 cup of the non-dairy topping.

Mound the filling into the crust. Cover lightly with foil. Freeze the yogurt lemon pie for 2 hours or until the pie is firm.

To serve, set pie on the counter at room temperature to soften slightly. Slice pie and serve.

This is a new twist to an old favorite pie. To crush candy canes, break canes into small pieces and crush in a food processor fitted with a steel blade or crush between two pieces of waxed paper using a rolling pin.

YOGURT MINT ALASKA PIE

SERVES 6

9-inch cookie crust, chilled

3 cups vanilla frozen yogurt

½ cup crushed candy canes

4 egg whites at room temperature

½ teaspoon cream of tartar

¼ cup sugar

Prepare cookie crust. Chill 20 minutes or longer.

Stir yogurt to soften. Mix in crushed candy canes. Spread yogurt in the cooled pie crust. Cover with foil and freeze until solid.

When ready to serve, beat egg whites with cream of tartar until soft peaks form. Sprinkle sugar over egg whites. Continue beating until stiff. Mound meringue over yogurt and spread to edges, completely sealing.

Set pie on cookie sheet. Bake pie in preheated 500°F. oven for 2½-3 minutes or until tips of meringue are golden brown. Serve immediately. Tastes great with a chocolate sauce.

CHILLED PEACH YOGURT PIE

≈

SERVES 6

8-inch gingersnap crust, chilled

1 cup chopped peaches

2 tablespoons freshly squeezed orange juice

2 tablespoons light brown sugar

3 cups peach yogurt

¼ teaspoon ground nutmeg

1½ cups non-dairy whipped topping or
   whipped cream

Prepare gingersnap crust. Refrigerate crust for 20 minutes or longer.

Toss peaches with orange juice and sugar in a deep bowl. Stir in yogurt. Blend in nutmeg and whipped topping.

Mound yogurt filling into crust. Cover lightly with foil. Freeze Peach Yogurt Pie for 2 hours or until pie is firm. To serve, set pie on counter at room temperature to soften slightly before serving.

For this pie, plain yogurt is strained through cheesecloth for one day. The result is a slightly tart yogurt cheese which works perfectly in this recipe.

R UM RAISIN
YOGURT CHEESE PIE

SERVES 6

5 cups plain yogurt

9-inch nut crust, unbaked

1 cup golden raisins

¼ cup dark rum

½ cup sour cream

½ cup firmly packed light brown sugar

4 eggs

½ teaspoon vanilla

Prepare nut crust and set aside.

Line a colander or other strainer with a double thickness of cheesecloth. Set over a bowl. Spoon yogurt into colander and cover with plastic wrap. Refrigerate overnight.

Roll out pastry dough. Set the dough in pie plate and pat down so that the dough fits securely. Crimp edges. Prick bottom and sides with tines of a fork. Line the dough with foil and set pie weights or dry beans on top. Bake in a 425°F. oven for 10 minutes. Remove foil and weights and bake 5 more minutes. Remove crust from the oven. Cool.

Plump raisins in the rum for 1 hour. Beat yogurt cheese with sour cream. Sprinkle half of the sugar over cheese and incorporate. Repeat until all the sugar has been used.

Add eggs, 1 at a time, beating well after each addition. Mix in rum and raisins and vanilla.

Spoon filling into crust. Bake in a 325°F. oven until pie tests done, about 1 hour. Cool on rack.

You can use other fruits or berries of the season if you wish.

RASPBERRY
FROZEN YOGURT PIE

SERVES 6

9-inch vanilla wafer crust, baked
1 quart fresh (or defrosted and drained)
   raspberries, picked over, washed, and set
   to dry on paper towels
½ cup sugar
2 cups vanilla yogurt
½ teaspoon vanilla

Prepare crust. Bake crust in a 375°F. oven for 5-7 minutes. The edges of crust will brown slightly. Cool crust before adding the filling.

Toss raspberries with sugar. Gently fold in yogurt and vanilla. Mixture will turn pink as you crush some of the berries.

Mound filling into the pie crust. Cover pie lightly with foil and freeze. Set pie at room temperature to soften slightly before serving.

CRISPS, CRUMBLES, COBBLERS, DOWDIES, BUCKLES, GRUNTS, AND SLUMPS

Apple Betty. Apple Betty is applesauce or sliced apples baked in a graham cracker crust. My mother would then sprinkle a layer of graham cracker crumbs over the top of the Apple Betty and serve it spooned into a shallow dessert dish and topped with sweetened whipped cream.

Apple Pandowdy. An apple pandowdy is a single crust apple pie, but the top crust is cut and mixed in with the apples during the last few minutes of the baking time.

Buckle. A buckle is a layer of fruit covered with a cake batter or a crumb topping. It tends to "buckle" as it bakes.

Crisps. This dessert favorite uses baked fruit, topped with a mixture of oats and brown sugar.

Crumbles. A crumble consists of baked fruit with a streusel topping, cooked to perfection. The name certainly derives from the "crumbly" topping.

Roly Poly. This is similar to a jelly roll, but it is filled with stewed fruit.

Dowdies. The term *dowdies* may derive from the practice of cutting up the top crust of this dish, which is then "dowdied," or pushed into the pie itself.

Slump. A slump is fruit and biscuit with dumplings. After the fruit is cooked or baked the complete dessert is turned upside down. The biscuits open easily with a fork or spoon and the fruit is slumped into the biscuits.

Cobbler. This dessert resembles a slump in that it is a dessert of cooked fruit with a biscuit dough dumpling, but the cobbler is served from the dish. Does the sight of biscuits on the fruit remind you of cobblestones? Perhaps that is how this dish received its name.

Grunt. A grunt is a cobbler cooked on top of the stove. Its name comes from the sounds it makes while cooking. For best results, always use the highest quality ripe fruit.

The popularity of fruit desserts blossomed in the early days of New England. It was a natural and creative style in which to utilize the abundant fruit harvest. I remember fondly how my father and brother picked apples from the trees each fall from our garden. My mother was waiting in the kitchen to tend the harvest.

APPLE PANDOWDY

SERVES 6

PASTRY DOUGH

1⅛ cups unbleached all-purpose flour

½ teaspoon salt

⅓ cup lard or vegetable shortening

3 to 4 tablespoons ice water

FILLING

2¼ pounds cooking apples, such as
   Granny Smiths

1 cup sugar

¾ teaspoon ground cinnamon

¼ teaspoon salt

3 tablespoons flour

¼ teaspoon ground mace

3 tablespoons butter or margarine

To prepare pastry combine the flour and the salt. Cut lard or vegetable shortening into the flour. Mixture will resemble coarse meal. Sprinkle water, a tablespoon at a time, over the dough. Mix and add enough water so that the dough clings together. Shape into a dough ball. Wrap dough in plastic wrap and refrigerate 1 hour. (Dough can be prepared a day before using.) Roll out dough to fit over a 1-quart casserole.

Peel, core, and slice the apples. Mix together sugar, cinnamon, salt, flour, and mace. Crumble in butter. Toss apples with sugar mixture.

Arrange apples in greased casserole. Carefully set pastry over apples. Allow crust to slightly hang over the edge of dish yet press crust firmly to dish. Flute edges and make a ½-inch steam vent in the center.

Bake pandowdy in a 425°F. oven for 30 minutes. Reduce heat to 350°F. Break up crust with the back of a spoon, turning it and the apples over. Continue baking for 8-10 minutes. Serve Apple Pandowdy hot or warm. Good with cream or yogurt.

Apple Betty is apple sauce or sliced apples baked in a graham cracker crust.

APPLE BETTY

❧

SERVES 6

GRAHAM CRACKER CRUST

1½ cups graham cracker crumbs

½ cup granulated sugar

¼ cup butter or margarine, melted

½ teaspoon ground cinnamon

FILLING

4½ cups thinly sliced apples

2 teaspoons freshly squeezed lemon juice

¾ cup firmly packed light brown sugar

¼ cup unbleached all-purpose flour

¾ teaspoon ground cinnamon

¼ teaspoon ground mace

⅓ cup butter or margarine, melted

Toss graham cracker crumbs with granulated sugar, ½ teaspoon cinnamon, and ¼ cup melted butter in a deep bowl. Pat crumbs into a 9-inch pie plate. Set aside.

Toss apple slices with lemon juice, brown sugar, flour, cinnamon, mace, and remaining butter. Place apples in pie plate.

Bake Apple Betty in a 375°F. oven for 25 minutes or until apples are fork tender. Apple Betty is best served warm. It is good with vanilla ice cream or vanilla yogurt.

APPLE BETTY
WITH APPLE SAUCE

SERVES 6

4 cups apple sauce

9-inch graham cracker crust (see page 140)

1½ cups graham cracker crumbs

3 tablespoons sugar

½ teaspoon ground cinnamon

¼ cup butter or margarine, melted

Spoon apple sauce into prepared graham cracker crust. Toss remaining graham cracker crumbs with sugar, cinnamon, and butter. Sprinkle over apple sauce.

Bake Apple Betty in a 350°F. oven for 25-30 minutes. Serve Apple Betty warm. Good with cream or vanilla yogurt.

Baked fruit is topped with an oat and brown sugar mixture.

CHERRY CRISP

SERVES 6-8

1 cup quick-cooking rolled oats

¾ cup firmly packed light brown sugar

½ cup unbleached all-purpose flour

1 teaspoon ground cinnamon

¼ teaspoon ground cardamom seeds

6 tablespoons butter or margarine

4 cups fresh or frozen cherries (if frozen,
   defrost and drain)

Toss oats, sugar, cinnamon, and cardamom. Cut in butter. Arrange cherries in a greased 8-inch square pan. Sprinkle topping over cherries.

Bake Cherry Crisp at 375°F. for 30 minutes or until the topping is a golden color. Serve warm with ice cream or yogurt.

A buckle is a layer of fruit covered with a cake batter and a crumb topping. It tends to "buckle" as it bakes. As is the rule with so many of these dishes, different berries can be combined to create buckles using the freshest available ingredients.

BLUEBERRY BUCKLE

SERVES 6

2½-3 cups picked-over fresh blueberries
  (or frozen, defrosted, drained blueberries),
  divided
2 tablespoons unbleached, all-purpose flour
¼ cup butter or margarine
¾ cup sugar
1 egg
½ cup milk
2 cups unbleached all-purpose flour
1¾ teaspoons baking powder
¼ teaspoon salt
¼ cup sugar
1 teaspoon ground cinnamon
1 teaspoon ground nutmeg

Toss blueberries with 2 tablespoons of flour. Place in bottom of greased 8½-inch baking pan or pie plate.

Cream butter and sugar until light. Mix in egg and milk. Blend in flour, baking powder, and salt. Spoon batter over top of berries.

Combine sugar, cinnamon, and nutmeg. Sprinkle over top of batter.

Bake in a 375°F. oven for 40-45 minutes or until cake tester comes out clean. Serve warm with ice cream or frozen yogurt.

APPLE RASPBERRY CRISP

SERVES 8

2 cups fresh or defrosted and drained
   raspberries
2 pounds cooking apples, peeled, cored, and
   sliced
1 cup quick-cooking oats
½ cup unbleached all-purpose flour
¾ cup firmly packed light brown sugar
¼ teaspoon salt
¾ teaspoon ground cinnamon
¼ teaspoon ground mace
½ cup butter or margarine at room
   temperature

Toss berries and apples together. Arrange fruit in a greased 9 x 9-inch baking dish.

Mix oats, flour, sugar, salt, cinnamon, and mace together. Cut butter into oat mixture. Sprinkle oat mixture over fruit.

Bake in a 375°F. oven for 25-30 minutes or until golden on top. Serve warm. Good with ice cream or yogurt.

Roly Poly is similar to a jelly roll, but filled with stewed fruit.

Strawberry Roly Poly

❧

SERVES 6

2¼ cups unbleached all-purpose flour

1 teaspoon baking soda

¼ teaspoon salt

3 tablespoons sugar

¼ cup vegetable shortening

⅔ cup milk

2½ cups hulled strawberries, mashed

¼ cup butter, cut in ½-inch pieces

¾ cup sugar

Mix together flour, baking powder, salt, and 3 tablespoons sugar. Cut in shortening, using a pastry knife or food processor fitted with a steel blade. Blend in milk. Turn dough onto a lightly floured board; roll dough ¼ inch thick.

Spread dough with strawberries and sprinkle with butter and sugar. Roll dough jelly-roll style. Place on lightly greased cookie sheet.

Bake in a 350°F. oven for 35 minutes. Cake will test done. Cool 5 minutes. Transfer roly poly to serving dish. Slice and serve.

A crumble is baked fruit with a streusel topping and cooked to perfection.

PEACH CRUMBLE

SERVES 6

4 cups peeled, sliced peaches

½ cup firmly packed light brown sugar

2 tablespoons freshly squeezed orange juice

2 tablespoons cornstarch

⅓ cup butter or margarine, cut in ½-inch
   pieces

1 cup unbleached all-purpose flour

½ cup granulated sugar

1 teaspoon grated orange peel

Toss the sliced peaches with brown sugar and orange juice. Arrange peach slices in a buttered 9 x 9-inch baking pan.

Cut the butter into the flour. Mix with granulated sugar and orange peel. Sprinkle streusel over the peaches.

Bake Peach Crumble in a 350°F. oven for 35 minutes or until the fruit is tender. Spoon crumble into sauce dishes and serve with cream, ice cream, or vanilla yogurt.

A slump is fruit and biscuit dumpling. After the fruit is cooked (or baked), the complete dessert is turned upside down. The biscuits open easily with a fork or spoon, and the fruit is slumped into it.

STRAWBERRY SLUMP

SERVES 6

6 cups hulled strawberries, cut in half

¾ cup sugar

3 tablespoons cornstarch

1 cup water

1 cup unbleached all-purpose flour

1½ teaspoons baking powder

½ cup milk

In a saucepan toss strawberries with sugar, cornstarch, and water. Bring mixture to a boil. Reduce to simmer and cook 5 minutes, stirring often. Spoon mixture into 9 x 9-inch baking pan. Bake in 350°F. oven for 5 minutes.

Meanwhile, mix flour, baking powder, and milk in a bowl. Using hot pads, remove fruit mixture from oven and drop biscuit dough directly onto fruit. Cover and continue cooking for 15 minutes. Remove cover and bake 5 minutes longer.

To serve, spoon a biscuit onto a dessert dish, open biscuit, and spoon fruit onto biscuit. Serve hot.

CHERRY SLUMP

SERVES 6

5 cups pitted sour cherries, picked over,
 washed, and drained
½ cup sugar
1 tablespoon grated lemon peel
1 tablespoon freshly squeezed lemon juice
3 tablespoons cornstarch
1 cup water
1 cup unbleached all-purpose flour
1½ teaspoons baking powder
½ cup milk
1 tablespoon grated lemon peel

In a saucepan toss cherries with sugar, peel, juice, and cornstarch
mixed with water. Bring mixture to a boil, over medium heat, stirring
often. Pour cherries into a 9 x 9-inch baking dish. Bake in 350°F. oven
for 15 minutes.

Mix flour and baking powder in a bowl. Stir in milk and lemon
peel. Using a tablespoon, shape dumplings and spoon over fruit.
Cover and cook 15 minutes. Remove cover and cook 5 minutes.

To serve, spoon a biscuit onto a dessert dish, open biscuit, and
spoon fruit onto biscuit. Serve hot.

A cobbler resembles a slump in that it is a dessert of cooked fruit with a biscuit dough dumpling, but the cobbler is served from the dish. Does the sight of biscuits on the fruit remind you of cobblestones? Perhaps that is how this dish received its name.

APRICOT COBBLER

SERVES 6

6 cups sliced and pitted apricots

½ cup sugar

2 tablespoons cornstarch

1½ cups unbleached all-purpose flour, sifted

1½ teaspoons baking powder

⅛ teaspoon salt

¼ cup vegetable shortening

½ cup milk, or enough milk to make a soft
   dough

Toss apricots with sugar and cornstarch. Spoon fruit into a 1-quart greased baking dish.

Mix flour, baking powder, and salt in a bowl. Cut in vegetable shortening. Stir in enough milk to make a soft dough. Using a tablespoon, shape dumplings over fruit.

Bake the cobbler at 375°F. for 35-40 minutes, or until the dumplings are a golden brown. Remove cobbler from oven and serve warm. Good with vanilla ice cream.

INDIVIDUAL CRANBERRY COBBLERS

SERVES 6

1 cup sugar

¾ cup water

½ cup freshly squeezed orange juice, divided

1 package (12 ounces) fresh cranberries, washed and picked over, bruised or dried berries discarded

3 cups chopped and cored pears

¼ cup freshly squeezed orange juice

1½ cups unbleached all-purpose flour, sifted

1½ teaspoons baking powder

⅛ teaspoon salt

¼ cup vegetable shortening

½ cup milk, or enough milk to make a soft dough

Blend sugar with water and ¼ cup orange juice in a saucepan. Cook mixture over medium heat until it comes to a boil. Stir in cranberries. Again bring mixture to a boil. Reduce heat to medium and continue cooking for 10 minutes, stirring occasionally. Cool stewed cranberries.

Combine cranberries and pears with remaining orange juice. Spoon fruit evenly into 6 greased ramekins or custard cups.

Mix flour, baking powder, and salt in a bowl. Cut in vegetable shortening. Stir in enough milk to make a soft dough. Using a tablespoon, shape a dumpling on each ramekin.

Bake cobblers in a 375° F. oven for 30 minutes or until biscuits are golden brown. Remove cobbler from oven and serve warm.

A *"grunt" is a simmered cobbler with dumplings on top. Its name comes from the sounds it makes while cooking. This dish is cooked on top of the stove.*

BERRY GRUNT

SERVES 6

3 cups fresh (or defrosted and drained)
   raspberries and/or blueberries
1 cup water
½ cup plus 2 tablespoons sugar
1½ cups unbleached all-purpose flour
1½ teaspoons baking powder
¼ teaspoon ground nutmeg
¼ teaspoon salt
⅔ cup buttermilk

Stir berries, water, and sugar together in saucepan. Simmer for 5 minutes, stirring often.

Meanwhile combine flour, baking powder, nutmeg, and salt. Blend in buttermilk; do not overmix. Drop batter over berries, making 6 dumplings. Cover and simmer 8-10 minutes.

Serve berries hot in a small dish with a dumpling.

For best results, always use highest quality and ripest fruit available. A grunt is fruit simmered in a saucepan with a layer of biscuit dough. If you listen closely, you can hear it "grunt" while cooking.

PEAR GRUNT

SERVES 6

2 cups biscuit flour

½ cup milk

2 tablespoons grated orange peel, divided

6 cups cored and chopped pears

½ cup sugar

½ teaspoon ground cinnamon

1 cup water

3 tablespoons cornstarch

Mix biscuit flour, milk, and 1 tablespoon orange peel; set aside.

In a frying pan, mix pear pieces, remaining orange peel, sugar, cinnamon, water, and cornstarch. Bring mixture to a boil, reduce heat to simmer, and cook 5 minutes. Stir occasionally.

Increase heat to medium and spoon biscuit dough onto pears. Cover and cook 10 minutes. Spoon grunt onto sauce dishes and serve hot.

WINTER PIES

Winter pies, often prepared after the close of the fresh fruit and berry seasons, make use of ingredients that can be easily obtained even when the land, orchard, and berry patches are frozen up and snowed over. These pieces include lemon nut pies, nut pies, raisin pies, and mincemeat pies. Obviously, these pies can be made in any season and are always delicious; however, they are well adapted to the winter kitchen. I have included recipes for mincemeat pie and peanut butter pie in this section. Mince pie is a natural for using winter nuts and raisins.

CHESS PIE

SERVES 6

8-inch single pie crust, unbaked

5 tablespoons dry sherry

1¼ cup currants

6 tablespoons butter or margarine

1 cup sugar

2 eggs

¼ cup heavy cream

¾ cup chopped walnuts or pecans

½ teaspoon vanilla

Roll out pastry dough to about an 11-inch circle. Set the dough in pie plate, patting the dough with finger tips until it covers the edges of the pan. Firm down the edges of the crust. Crimp edges. Set aside.

Pour sherry into a small bowl, mix in currants, and let stand for 20 minutes.

Beat butter and sugar until light. Add eggs one at a time, beating well after each addition. Mix in cream, sherry, currants, walnuts, and vanilla.

Pour batter into pie crust. Bake pie in a 350°F. oven for 40 minutes or until pie tests done. Cool pie on rack. Chess pie is best served at room temperature.

Cinnamon, nutmeg, and mace are the three most commonly used spices with which to flavor pies. These spices are popular because they marry well with fruit and impart a delicious complementary flavor to fruit pies.

Cinnamon has a pungent, slightly bittersweet flavor. Nutmeg has a warm, spicy, sweet flavor. Mace is produced from the membrane of the nutmeg seed, and it tastes like a slightly more pungent version of nutmeg.

VERMONT CIDER PIE

SERVES 6

9-inch lattice (double) pie crust, unbaked
2 cups sweet apple cider
½ cup sugar
⅓ cup unbleached all-purpose flour
½ teaspoon ground cinnamon
2 eggs
2 tablespoons butter or margarine
1 egg white
Sugar for topping

Roll out pastry dough into an 11-inch circle. Set the dough in pie plate and pat down so that dough fits securely. Press dough so that it extends just past the edges of the pie plate. Firm down edges and crimp. Set aside.

Combine cider and sugar in saucepan. Cook over medium heat until mixture comes to a boil, stirring often. In a small bowl, mix ½ cup of the cider mixture with the flour. Beat eggs until light. In a slow steady stream, stir flour and eggs into cider mixture. Continue cooking until filling is slightly thickened, about 2-3 minutes. Cool. Whisk in butter.

Pour filling into pie crust. Roll out extra crust and cut into strips. Set on top of pie in lattice arrangement. Brush top of crust with egg whites and sprinkle with sugar.

Bake pie in a 350°F. oven for 40-45 minutes or until crust is golden brown and pie tests done.

Eggnog Pie
with Ginger Cream

SERVES 6

9-inch single nut pastry crust, unbaked

EGGNOG CUSTARD

4 eggs

½ cup sugar

¼ teaspoon salt

2 cups milk, scalded and cooled

¼ cup dark rum

2 teaspoons brandy

1 teaspoon vanilla

¼ teaspoon ground nutmeg

¼ teaspoon ground cinnamon

GINGER CREAM

1 cup heavy cream, chilled

⅓ cup sugar

½ teaspoon vanilla

**⅓ cup minced candied ginger or preserved
   ginger**

Roll out pastry dough to about an 11-inch circle. Set the dough in pie plate, patting the dough with finger tips until it covers the edges of the pan. Firm down the edges of the crust. Crimp edges. Set aside.

Beat eggs, ½ cup sugar, and salt until light. Mix 3 tablespoons of the egg mixture into the cooled milk. In a slow steady stream pour the milk into the egg mixture. Blend in rum, brandy, 1 teaspoon vanilla, nutmeg, and cinnamon.

Pour custard into the pie crust. Bake in the center of a 400°F. oven for 10 minutes. Lower the heat to 350°F. and continue baking for 30 minutes or until the pie tests done. A knife inserted in the center of the pie will come out clean. Cool pie on rack. Serve cold with Ginger Cream.

Just before serving time make the Ginger Cream. Beat the cream until soft peaks form. Sprinkle with sugar. Continue beating until sugar is incorporated and firm peaks form. Blend in vanilla and candied ginger.

LEMON NUT PIE

SERVES 6

9-inch single pie crust, unbaked

4 egg yolks

⅔ cup sugar

3 tablespoons grated lemon peel

2 tablespoons freshly squeezed lemon juice

1¼ cups ground almonds

2 tablespoons cornstarch

4 egg whites, beaten stiff

Roll out pastry dough to an 11-inch circle. Place dough in a pie plate, patting the dough with your fingers until it extends just past the edges of the pie plate. Firm down edges. Set aside.

Beat egg yolks and sugar until light. Stir in peel, juice, almonds, and cornstarch. Fold in egg whites.

Pour batter into unbaked pie shell. Bake pie in center of oven at 350°F. for 30 minutes or until lightly brown or until pie tests done.

Remove pie from oven and cool on rack. Decorate pie with candied lemon slices.

MAPLE SUGAR PIE

SERVES 6

9-inch single pie crust, unbaked

2 cups milk

¼ teaspoon mace

3 eggs

1 egg yolk

⅓ cup pure maple sugar

¾ teaspoon vanilla

1 cup golden raisins

Roll out pastry dough to an 11-inch circle. Set the dough in pie plate and pat down so that dough fits securely. Firm down edges and crimp. Set aside.

Scald milk together with mace. Cool and set aside. Meanwhile, beat the eggs and yolk. Mix in the maple sugar.

Mix 2 tablespoons of the milk into eggs. In a slow steady stream, stir eggs into cooled milk. Mix in vanilla and raisins.

Pour maple sugar filling into pie crust. Bake the pie in a 375°F. oven for 45 minutes or until a knife inserted in center of pie comes out clean. Cool pie on rack. Serve cold.

In August 1990 we spent time at Hancock Village with our good friends, Maureen and Shelly Tobin. I am grateful for their introducing us to the Shaker community.

BUTTERNUT MAPLE PIE

SERVES 6

9-inch single pie crust, unbaked

3 eggs

¼ teaspoon salt

2 tablespoons cornstarch

2 cups cooked, mashed butternut squash

⅓ cup maple syrup

1½ cups half-and-half, scalded and cooled

¾ teaspoon ground cinnamon

¼ teaspon ground nutmeg

¼ teaspoon ground ginger

Roll out pastry dough to about an 11-inch circle. Set the dough in pie plate, patting the dough with finger tips until it covers the edges of the pan. Firm down the edges of the crust. Crimp edges. Set aside.

Beat eggs with salt and cornstarch until light. Blend in squash and maple syrup. Mix 3 tablespoons of the egg into the half-and-half and then in a slow steady stream mix half-and-half into the eggs. Stir in cinnamon, nutmeg, and ginger.

Pour filling into the pie crust. Bake pie in the center of a 450°F. oven for 10 minutes. Lower the heat to 325°F. and continue baking for 30 minutes or until the pie tests done. A knife inserted in the center of the pie will come out clean.

Cool pie on rack. Serve pie cold or at room temperature.

ALL FRUIT
MINCEMEAT PIE

9-inch double pie crust, unbaked (p. 94)

All Fruit Mincemeat (p. 162)

2 tablespoons milk

BRANDY HARD SAUCE

1½ cups confectioner's sugar

½ cup butter or margarine

1 teaspoon vanilla

¼ teaspoon ground nutmeg

3 tablespoons brandy

Roll out pastry dough to an 11-inch circle. Set the dough in pie plate and pat down so that dough fits securely and extends just past the edges of the pie plate. Firm down the edges of the crust. Set aside.

Mound 5 cups of mincemeat filling into pastry crust. Reserve any extra filling for cookies.

Roll out remaining dough. Cut small hole in center of pastry. Set pastry on top of pie, trim edges, leaving small overhang. Fold edges under and crimp to seal. Cover edges of pie with foil to prevent burning. Brush top of pie with milk.

Bake pie in a 375°F. oven for 40-50 minutes or until crust is a golden brown. Remove foil after 20 minutes. Cool pie on rack. Serve pie cold with Brandy Hard Sauce.

To prepare Hard Sauce, cream butter with sugar in food processor fitted with steel blade. Add vanilla, nutmeg, and brandy. Blend.

Spoon into a serving crock and refrigerate until needed. Let sauce stand at room temperature 20 minutes to soften before serving on pie.

ALL FRUIT MINCEMEAT

❧

MAKES 1¼ QUARTS

½ small lemon

1 small navel orange

3 cups diced apples

1 cup chopped walnuts

1½ cups golden raisins

1 cup mixed diced candied fruits

½ cup orange juice

2 cups firmly packed light brown sugar

¾ tablespoon ground cinnamon

½ teaspoon ground nutmeg

½ teaspoon ground cloves

½ teaspoon ground allspice

½ teaspoon salt

½ cup plus 1 tablespoon good quality brandy

Cut lemon and orange in quarters, discard seeds, and grind in food processor or grinder.

Combine ground lemon and orange with apples, nuts, raisins, fruit, and juice. In a saucepan, bring mixture to a boil. Reduce heat to a simmer and continue cooking for 10 minutes, stirring occasionally. Add sugar, cinnamon, nutmeg, cloves, allspice, and salt. Cook 15 minutes, stirring often. Stir in brandy and continue cooking until mincemeat is thick, about 10-15 minutes.

Cool. Spoon into bowl. Cover and store in refrigerator for 3-4 days.

During the baking process this pie forms its "own" top crust.

OATMEAL NUT PIE

SERVES 6

9-inch single pie crust, unbaked

¼ cup butter or margarine, melted and cooled

¾ cup sugar

¼ teaspoon ground cinnamon

¼ teaspoon ground nutmeg

¼ teaspoon ground allspice

½ cup ground walnuts or pecans

¾ cup dark corn syrup

3 eggs

1 cup quick-cooking rolled oats

Roll out pastry dough to about an 11-inch circle. Set the dough in pie plate, patting the dough with finger tips until it covers the edges of the pan. Firm down the edges of the crust. Crimp edges. Set aside.

Cream the butter and sugar. Mix in spices and nuts. Blend in corn syrup. Beat in eggs, 1 at a time, beating well after each addition. Mix in oats. Spoon filling into prepared crust.

Bake the oatmeal pie in the center of a 350°F. oven for 1 hour or until the pie tests done. Cool on rack. Serve warm or room temperature.

PEANUT BUTTER PIE

SERVES 6

9-inch single peanut crust, baked (see p. 92)

(see p. 92)

1¾ cups milk

¼ cup butter or margarine

½ cup sugar

¼ teaspoon salt

¼ cup cornstarch

½ cup water

4 egg yolks, beaten

⅓ cup good quality smooth peanut butter

1 cup chopped peanuts

Roll out the pastry dough to an 11-inch circle. Place the dough in a pie plate, patting the dough with your fingers until it extends just past the edge of the rim of the pan. Firm down the edges of the crust. Prick the crust in several places and set a sheet of aluminum foil over the crust, pressing it down against the dough to help the dough keep its shape during baking. Cover foil with pie weights or dry beans. Bake crust in the center of a 425°F. oven for 10 minutes. Remove foil and weights and bake 5 more minutes. Remove crust from the oven. Cool.

In a saucepan combine milk, butter, sugar, and salt and bring to boil over medium heat. Cool. Blend cornstarch and water together and stir in eggs. In a slow steady stream, add to milk mixture, stirring constantly. Continue cooking until mixture thickens, stirring often.

Remove filling from heat. Stir in peanut butter. Cool. Sprinkle pie with chopped nuts. Serve with sweetened whipped cream or vanilla yogurt if desired.

What Thanksgiving feast would be complete without the following recipe?

PECAN PIE

SERVES 6

9-inch single pie crust, unbaked

3 eggs

1 cup dark corn syrup

½ cup firmly packed light brown sugar

3 tablespoons butter, melted and cooled

1 teaspoon vanilla

2 teaspoons dark rum

½ teaspoon ground cinnamon

1¾ cups pecans

Roll out pastry dough into an 11-inch circle. Set the dough in pie plate and pat down so that dough fits securely in pie plate and extends just past the edge of the plate. Firm down edges of crust. Set aside.

Beat eggs lightly. Mix in corn syrup, sugar, butter, vanilla, rum, and cinnamon. Stir in pecans. Pour the filling into the crust.

Bake pecan pie at 325°F. for 35 minutes or until filling tests done. Cool pie on rack and serve. Good with whipped cream.

PRUNE WHIP PIE

SERVES 6

**9-inch single walnut crunch crust, baked
   (see p. 92)**
1½ cups cooked, pitted prunes, drained
2 tablespoons grated lemon peel
1½ cups minced pitted prunes
2 tablespoons orange flavor liqueur
¾ cup ground walnuts
2 cups chilled heavy cream, whipped
½ cup sugar

Roll out the pastry dough to an 11-inch circle. Place the dough in a pie plate, patting the dough with your fingers until it extends just past the edge of the rim of the pan. Firm down the edges of the crust. Prick the crust in several places and set a sheet of aluminum foil over the crust, pressing it down against the dough to help the dough keep its shape during baking. Cover foil with pie weights or dry beans. Bake crust in the center of a 425°F. oven for 10 minutes. Remove foil and weights and bake 5 more minutes. Remove crust from the oven. Cool.

Purée drained prunes with lemon peel in food processor fitted with steel blade. Remove purée and spoon into a bowl.

Marinate minced prunes with liqueur for 15 minutes. Mix prunes with purée. Stir in walnuts and whipped cream mixed with sugar.

Mound prune filling into prepared crust. Refrigerate until serving time. Serve pie cold.

SQUASH PIE

SERVES 6

9-inch single pie crust, unbaked

2½ cups fresh or defrosted squash, steamed
  and strained

¾ cup sugar

1 teaspoon salt

½ teaspoon ground cinnamon

½ teaspoon ground ginger

½ teaspoon ground nutmeg

1 egg (use 2 eggs if they are small, and then
  cut down on milk by about ¼ cup)

1¾ cups milk

Roll out the pastry dough to a 10-inch circle. Place dough in a pie plate, patting the dough with your fingers until it extends just past the edge of the rim of the pan. Build up the sides of crust so that the filling will not overflow.

In a large bowl mix squash, sugar, salt, and spices. Gradually blend in the slightly beaten egg and milk. Strain the filling into prepared crust.

Bake the pie in the center of a 425°F. oven for 15-20 minutes. Crust will be a golden brown around the edges. Reduce heat to 350°F. and continue baking until a knife inserted in the center of the pie comes out clean, about 25 minutes. Cool pie on rack. Best served warm.

"The glory of the pumpkin is the pie." If you are preparing fresh pumpkin, freeze extra pulp for your next pie.

PUMPKIN PIE WITH STREUSEL TOPPING

SERVES 6

9-inch single orange flavored pie crust,
  unbaked
3 eggs, beaten
2 cups baked pulp from peeled pumpkin or
  1 can (12 ounces) prepared pumpkin
  filling
¾ cup granulated sugar
¼ teaspoon salt
¼ teaspoon fresh grated ginger
¼ teaspoon ground cloves
¼ teaspoon ground nutmeg
1 teaspoon ground cinnamon
1 cup evaporated milk

STREUSEL TOPPING

1 cup unbleached all-purpose flour
½ cup firmly packed light brown sugar
¼ cup butter or margarine, cut in small
  pieces

Roll out pastry dough into an 11-inch circle. Set the dough in pie plate and pat down so that the dough fits securely. Press dough so that it extends just past the edges of the pie plate. Set aside.

Blend eggs and pumpkin together. Mix in sugar and remaining ingredients. Pour pumpkin filling into the crust.

To prepare struesel topping mix together flour, sugar, and butter bits.

Cover the edges of pastry with aluminum foil strips to prevent scorching. Bake pie in a 400°F. oven for 10 minutes. Sprinkle pie with streusel topping. Reduce heat to 325°F. and continue baking for 40 minutes or until the pie tests done. Remove foil after 20 minutes of baking. Cool pie on rack. Serve with whipped cream. Serve pie chilled.

BOILED RAISIN PIE

SERVES 6

9-inch lattice crust, unbaked
2½ cups dark raisins, washed and drained
2 cups water
1 cup sugar
¼ cup unbleached all-purpose flour
2 tablespoons white vinegar
3 tablespoons butter or margarine
¼ teaspoon ground mace
1 egg white
Sugar

Prepare crust as for a double crust. Roll out bottom pastry dough to about an 11-inch circle. Set the dough in pie plate, patting the dough with finger tips until it covers the edges of the crust. Crimp edges. Set aside.

Mix the raisins in the 2 cups of water in a saucepan. Bring mixture to a boil over medium heat. Reduce heat to simmer and continue cooking 6-8 minutes, stirring occasionally.

Meanwhile, in a small bowl combine 1 cup sugar and flour. Remove ¼ cup of the liquid from raisins and whisk into sugar mixture. Stir sugar into raisins. Continue simmering 5 minutes longer, stirring often until mixture thickens. Remove pan from heat. Mix in vinegar, butter, and mace. Cool filling and pour into the crust.

Roll out the top crust on a lightly floured board and cut into ½-inch strips using a sharp knife. Set half of the strips 1 inch apart over the raisin pie, twisting the strips slightly for a twirled effect. Starting at the center of the pie, place 1 strip of dough over the filling in the opposite direction of the other dough strips. Weave the pie crust strips through the other strips on the pie. Continue adding and weaving the strips until the lattice design is complete. Press the strip ends firmly to the bottom crust. Brush lattice crust with egg white and sprinkle with sugar.

Bake pie in a 400°F. oven for 30-35 minutes. Crust will be a golden brown. Cool pie on rack. Serve pie warm or cold.

SOUR CREAM RAISIN PIE

9-inch single pie crust, unbaked

1 cup sour cream

¾ cup sugar

1½ tablespoons cornstarch

2 egg yolks, lightly beaten

1 tablespoon grated lemon peel

¼ teaspoon ground allspice

1¼ cups dark raisins

3 egg whites at room temperature

¼ teaspoon cream of tartar

⅓ cup of sugar

Roll out pastry dough to an 11-inch circle. Set the dough in pie plate and pat down so that dough fits securely. Crimp edges. Set aside.

In a mixing bowl combine sour cream, ¾ cup sugar, and cornstarch. Blend in eggs, peel, allspice, and raisins. Spread filling into the prepared crust.

Bake pie in a 350°F. oven for 35-40 minutes or until it tests done. Cool pie on rack.

To prepare meringue, beat egg whites and cream of tartar until soft peaks form. Sprinkle half of the sugar over meringue and incorporate. Repeat the process and continue to beat until stiff peaks form. Mound meringue over cooled pie, being sure to seal the edges.

Bake pie in a 350°F. oven for 10-12 minutes or until peaks on pie are golden brown. Serve pie cool or at room temperature.

SHOO-FLY PIE

SERVES 6

9-inch single pie crust, unbaked

STREUSEL

1½ cups unbleached all-purpose flour

¾ cup firmly packed light brown sugar

½ teaspoon ground cinnamon

¼ teaspoon ground nutmeg

**6 tablespoons butter or margarine, cut in
    small pieces**

MOLASSES FILLING

½ teaspoon baking soda

½ cup molasses

½ cup boiling water

Roll out pastry dough to an 11-inch circle. Place dough in a pie plate, patting the dough with your fingers until it extends just past the edge of the rim of the pan. Firm down edge of crust. Set aside.

Mix together flour, sugar, cinnamon, nutmeg, and butter until crumbly. Set aside.

In a separate bowl, stir baking soda into molasses. Stir in boiling water. Pour the molasses filling into crust. Sprinkle streusel over the top of the pie.

Bake Shoo-Fly Pie in a 375° F. oven for 45 minutes or until crust is golden brown and pie tests done. Shoo-Fly Pie is best when served warm.

This old family recipe was given to me by David Marion.

VINEGAR PIE

SERVES 6

9-inch pie crust, baked
1 cup sugar, divided
⅓ cup unbleached all-purpose flour
1 cup water
3 egg yolks
1½ tablespoons butter or margarine
½ teaspoon freshly squeezed lemon juice
¼ cup cider vinegar

Roll out the pastry dough to an 11-inch circle. Place the dough in a pie plate, patting the dough with your fingers until it extends just past the edge of the rim of the pan. Firm down the edges of the crust. Prick the crust in several places and set a sheet of aluminum foil over the crust, pressing it down against the dough. Cover foil with pie weights or dry beans. Bake crust in the center of a 425°F. oven for 10 minutes. Remove foil and weights and bake 5 more minutes. Remove crust from oven and cool.

Stir ½ cup of the sugar with flour in a saucepan. Blend in water and cook 15 to 20 minutes until mixture thickens, stirring almost constantly. Cool.

Beat egg yolks with remaining sugar until light. Stir into cooled flour mixture. Cook 3-4 minutes over low heat, stirring almost constantly. Blend in butter, juice, and vinegar. Cool filling.

Pour filling into crust. Bake in a 325°F. oven for 20 minutes. Cool on rack. Serve pie at room temperature.

CHOCOLATE PIES

These pies are perfect to satisfy the chocolate need in all of us. Chocolate was an early import into New England and became a favorite flavor in a variety of dessert dishes. Another strong contender for a national favorite dessert, along with the apple pie and chocolate chip cookies, must certainly be the brownie. The brownie was developed in the state of Maine, and I have included two recipes for brownie pies that I am sure will become family favorites.

Store chocolate in a moisture-free, cool area, about 60-75°F. Chocolate should be at room temperature before using.

Black Bottom Pie

SERVES 6-8

9-inch single pie crust, baked

¾ cup sugar

2 tablespoons cornstarch

4 egg yolks

2 cups milk, scalded and cooled

1 teaspoon vanilla

1 tablespoon rum

1½ ounces unsweetened chocolate, melted
**   and cooled**

1 package gelatin

¼ cup water

1 cup heavy cream, chilled and whipped

Roll out the pastry dough to an 11-inch circle. Place dough in a pie plate, patting the dough with your fingers until it extends just past the edge of the rim of the pan. Firm down the edges of the crust. Prick the crust in several places and set a sheet of aluminum foil over the crust, pressing it down against the dough to help the dough keep its shape during baking. Cover foil with pie weights or dry beans. Bake crust in the center of a 425°F. oven for 10 minutes. Remove foil and weights and bake 5 more minutes. Remove crust from the oven. Cool.

Mix sugar with cornstarch. Beat egg yolks with sugar mixture until light. Mix 3 tablespoons of the egg mixture into the cooled milk. In a slow steady stream, mix the milk into the eggs. Pour sauce into a saucepan and simmer over medium heat almost to the boil. Reduce heat to a simmer and continue cooking until sauce is smooth and thickens slightly. Blend in the vanilla and the rum.

Stir 1½ cups of the sauce into the chocolate and cool. Pour chocolate sauce into the pie crust. Set crust in the refrigerator.

Soften gelatin in ¼ cup of water for about 5 minutes. Place the cup in a saucepan with simmering water. Blend the gelatin until it is warm and clear. Stir the gelatin into the remaining custard. Fold in the whipped cream. Using a spatula, spread the custard over the chocolate filling in pie crust. Refrigerate pie for 2½ hours or until set. Serve pie cold.

It is the marshmallow sauce on top of a "Bailey's" sundae that inspired this recipe.

BOSTON BROWNIE
FUDGE PIE
WITH TWO SAUCES

SERVES 6

9-inch single pie crust, unbaked

2 squares unsweetened chocolate, cut in
   small pieces

¼ cup butter or margarine

¾ cup sugar

3 eggs

2 tablespoons corn syrup

1 teaspoon vanilla

¼ teaspoon salt

¾ cup unbleached all-purpose flour

½ teaspoon baking powder

8 scoops vanilla ice cream

CHOCOLATE SAUCE

3 squares semi-sweet chocolate, cut into
   small pieces

½ cup milk or half-and-half

¾ cup sugar

3½ tablespoons butter or margarine

1 teaspoon vanilla

MARSHMALLOW SAUCE

¼ pound marshmallows, cut in half with
   scissors
¼ cup milk or half-and-half

Roll out the pastry dough to an 11-inch circle. Place the dough in a pie plate, patting the dough with your fingers until it extends just past the edge of the rim of the pan. Firm down the edges of the crust. Set aside.

Melt the 2 squares chocolate and ¼ cup butter together. Cool. Mix in sugar, eggs, corn syrup, and vanilla. Stir in salt, flour, and baking powder.

Pour batter into pie shell. Bake in a 350°F. oven for about 20-25 minutes. Top crust will be firm and the batter should be slightly moist. Cool on rack.

To make Chocolate Sauce, melt remaining chocolate together with ½ cup milk, stirring until melted. Stir in sugar and butter and continue cooking until sauce thickens, about 4 minutes. Remove sauce from heat and stir in vanilla. Sauce is good hot or cold.

To prepare Marshmallow Sauce, stir marshmallows into remaining milk in top of a double boiler over simmering water. Stir sauce occasionally until marshmallows have melted. Serve warm.

Serve pie at room temperature or slightly warm, topped with vanilla ice cream. Offer a choice of the two sauces.

Imagine a rich heavenly brownie crust with a rum custard topping. This recipe is for the chocolate lover in all of us.

BROWNIE PIE

SERVES 8

¾ cup unbleached all-purpose flour

½ teaspoon baking powder

2 ounces unsweetened chocolate, cut in
　　small pieces

7 tablespoons butter

1 cup sugar

2 eggs

1 teaspoon vanilla

1 cup chopped walnuts

RUM CUSTARD TOPPING

5 egg yolks

1 cup sugar, divided

1 package unflavored gelatin

½ cup cold water

⅓ cup dark rum

1 cup heavy cream

Sift flour and baking powder. Set aside. Melt chocolate with butter and cool. Beat 1 cup sugar and 2 eggs until light. Stir in the chocolate mixture and the vanilla. Mix in the flour and walnuts.

Spoon the batter into a greased deep 9-inch pie plate. Bake in a 350°F. oven for 20-35 minutes or until a tester comes out almost dry. (The brownie should not be dry.) Cool.

Meanwhile, prepare topping. Beat the egg yolks and ¾ cup of the sugar until light. Stir gelatin into the cold water. Let stand for 5 minutes. Pour gelatin mixture into a small saucepan. Simmer until gelatin dissolves. Stir it into egg yolks and add rum, whisking until combined, about 5 minutes.

Whip heavy cream until it begins to thicken. Sprinkle with remaining sugar and continue beating until firm peaks form. Stir cream into the custard mixture. Pour rum custard over the cooled Brownie Pie. Refrigerate until firm, about 3 hours. Serve cold or at room temperature.

This chocolate pie is equally good in a meringue shell or baked pie crust.

CHOCOLATE PUDDING PIE

SERVES 6

MERINGUE SHELL

3 egg whites

¼ teaspoon cream of tartar

½ teaspoon vanilla

½ cup sugar

½ cup ground hazelnuts

CHOCOLATE FILLING

1½ ounces semisweet chocolate, chopped in
  small pieces

2 cups milk, divided

½ cup sugar

¼ tablespoon salt

¼ cup cornstarch

¼ teaspoon ground cinnamon

1 teaspoon vanilla

Beat egg whites, cream of tartar, and vanilla until soft peaks form. Sprinkle half of sugar over egg whites and beat to incorporate. Repeat process with remaining sugar. Beat until stiff peaks form. Fold in hazelnuts.

Transfer meringue into a greased 9-inch pie plate. Using the back of a spoon, spread meringue evenly over the bottom of pie plate, pushing meringue 2-3 inches above sides of plate to form crust.

Preheat oven to 250°F. and bake crust 1 hour. Turn off heat and allow crust to dry 1½ hours or until dry and firm.

Over medium-low heat, melt chocolate with 1½ cups of the milk, sugar, and salt, stirring often.

Whisk cornstarch into remaining milk. Whisk into pudding mixture. Continue cooking over medium low heat about 15 minutes or until mixture thickens, stirring almost constantly. Remove from heat and whisk in cinnamon and vanilla. Cool.

Spoon pudding into meringue shell and chill before serving.

DERBY PIE

SERVES 6

9-inch chocolate cookie pie crust, unbaked

¾ cup sugar

½ cup unbleached all-purpose flour

1 package (6 ounces) semisweet chocolate bits

7 tablespoons butter

2 eggs, well beaten

1 teaspoon vanilla

1 cup chopped walnuts or pecans

Prepare cookie crust and set aside.

Blend together the sugar and flour. Set aside. Add ½ of the chocolate to the butter. Melt butter mixture and cool. Combine sugar mixture with melted butter, remaining chocolate, eggs, vanilla, and walnuts.

Pour filling into the pie crust. Bake pie in 325°F. oven for 45 minutes or until the pie tests done. A knife inserted in the center of the pie will come out clean. Serve pie at room temperature. Good with sweetened whipped cream.

FUDGE PECAN PIE

SERVES 6-8

9-inch single pie crust, unbaked

5 tablespoons good quality cocoa

10 tablespoons sugar

3 eggs

¾ cup light corn syrup

5 tablespoons butter, melted and cooled

1 teaspoon vanilla

1½ cups chopped pecans

Roll out the pastry dough and fold into quarters. Place dough in a 9-inch pie plate, patting the dough with your fingers until it extends just past the edge of the rim of the pan. Set aside.

Mix cocoa and sugar. Stir in eggs and beat well. Blend in corn syrup. Stir in butter and vanilla. Continue mixing until the butter is combined into the batter. Mix in pecans.

Pour filling into the pie shell and bake at 350°F. for 35 minutes or until pie tests done. A cake tester inserted in the center of the pie will come out clean. Cool before serving.

MOCHA CHEESE PIE

SERVES 6-8

9-inch chocolate cookie crust, chilled

1 package (8-ounces) cream cheese at room
   temperature, cut in thirds

8 ounces cream-style cottage cheese

¾ cup sugar

3 eggs

2 tablespoons cornstarch

1 teaspoon vanilla

1 ounce semisweet chocolate, chopped

¼ cup strong coffee or espresso

2 tablespoons coffee liqueur

Prepare crumb crust and refrigerate.

Beat cream cheese with cottage cheese, sugar, eggs, and corn-starch until light, about 10 minutes with an electric mixer. Stir in vanilla.

Melt chocolate with the coffee and cool. Blend in coffee liqueur. Stir chocolate into cheese mixture. Pour filling into cookie crust.

Bake pie in a 325°F. oven, in the center of the rack, for 1 hour or until the pie tests done and it is firm to the touch. Turn off oven. Leave the pie in the oven for 1½ hours with the door closed. Remove the pie from the oven. Cool completely. Refrigerate at least 6 hours before serving.

Serve cold. Garnish with shaved chocolate if desired.

This recipe is from my friends at Season to Taste Books. Barry remembers this dessert as a favorite when vacationing at Martha's Vineyard.

RASPBERRY CHOCOLATE PIE

SERVES 6

9-inch orange crust, baked

6 ounces semisweet chocolate, melted and
  cooled

4 cups raspberries

½ cup sugar

2 tablespoons grated orange peel

⅓ cup currant jelly

1 tablespoon water

Roll out pastry dough. Set the dough in pie plate and pat down so that the dough fits securely. Crimp edges. Prick the crust in several places and set a sheet of aluminum foil over the crust, pressing it down against the dough to help the dough keep its shape during baking. Cover foil with pie weights or dry beans. Bake crust in the center of a 425°F. oven for 10 minutes. Remove foil and weights and bake 5 more minutes. Remove crust from the oven. Cool.

Melt chocolate and cool. Spread chocolate evenly over bottom of the crust. Wash and pick over raspberries, discarding any bruised berries. Drain on paper towels. Toss berries with sugar and orange peel. Arrange raspberries on warm chocolate, before the chocolate dries. Chill pie until chocolate is firm.

Before serving, melt jelly with water over medium heat, stirring often. Brush cooled jelly over berries. Serve pie cold with sweetened whipped cream or vanilla yogurt.

When is a pie not a pie? When it is two chocolate cookies that are sandwiched together with a marshmallow fluff filling.

WHOOPIE PIE

SERVES 8 (MAKES 16 SMALL PIES)

¾ cup granulated sugar

5 tablespoons vegetable shortening

1 egg

2 cups unbleached all-purpose flour

1½ teaspoons baking soda

⅓ cup cocoa

1 cup milk

MARSHMALLOW FILLING

½ cup sifted confectioner's sugar

⅓ cup vegetable shortening

½ cup marshmallow fluff

1 teaspoon vanilla

2 tablespoons margarine at room temperature

To make the cookies beat together the granulated sugar and 5 tablespoons shortening until light. Mix in egg. Combine separately the flour, baking soda, and cocoa. Add dry ingredients alternately with milk to the batter.

Drop batter by heaping tablespoons onto an ungreased or aluminum foil-lined cookie sheet. Bake cookies in a 425°F. oven for 7-8 minutes. Cookies will be firm to the touch. Cool cookies on rack.

To prepare the filling beat the confectioner's sugar and remaining shortening until smooth. Mix in marshmallow fluff, vanilla, and margarine.

To assemble the pies spread the filling on flat side of cookie. Sandwich with a top cookie. Set Whoopie Pies on dessert plate. Good at room temperature.

INDEX